Till a Hundred and Twenty Years

a memoir

Till a Hundred and Twenty Years

a memoir

Jo-Ann Middleman

EMESS PRESS, **Publisher**
SAN DIEGO

Published in 1995 by

Emess Press
4532 Benhurst Ave.
San Diego, CA 92122

Copyright © 1994 by Jo-Ann Middleman

All rights reserved. No part of this book may be used or reproduced in any manner whatsoever without written permission, except in the case of brief quotations embodied in critical articles or reviews.

An earlier version of this memoir originally appeared as the Summer 1994 issue of *Journal of Psychology and Judaism*, Kerry M. Olitzky, Special Issue Editor, Human Sciences Press, Inc., N.Y.

Library of Congress Catalog Card Number: 95-94698.

ISBN 0-9647771-0-X

SECOND EDITION

Printed in the United States of America

DEDICATION

To my mother, Mary:

Who always said she lacked courage, wisdom and humor...
But she was wrong.

Acknowledgments

Writing a book is a lot like having a baby. It's not something you do alone. I wish to thank Karen O'Connor, Connie Stockman, Janet Kunert, Al Christman, Sylvia Bal Somerville, Lesa Heebner, and Anne Valades, whose faith in me gave me faith in myself.

Thanks also to Marsh Cassady, Jim Kitchen, John Cullen, Ray McKewon, Glen Vecchione, Jill Limber, Nirmala Moorthy, Jak Koke, Herb Kuhlman, Linda Morefield, Betty Reeves, Art Specht, Scott Myrom, Barbara Sack and Louis Lento—my workshop buddies for their incisive imput.

Special thanks to Marilyn Heikoff, for *ootching* me out of my writing closet, and to Diane Estus for all her practical help.

A *shanem dank* to my mother, Mary Carson, for letting me *dray her kup*. And to my husband and helpmate, Stanley, who walks beside me all the way—mere words will never be enough.

Table of Contents

Author's Forward 1
Setting the Scene 3

"VEY IS MIR!" 7

Sarah 9
Bubby and the Butcher 13
Bubby and the Birthday Cake 15
Bubby Battles the Bulge 17
Bubby Goes by Johnson's 20
Bubby Buys a Chair 28
Bubby and Ma Bell 31
Bubby at the Bradford 38
Bubby and the Brisket 43
Bubby the Believer 46
Bubby Goes to Bay Shore 52

"IF WE LIVE AND NOTHING HAPPENS" 73

Sophia 75
Reel to Real 77
Supper with Aunt Sophia 83

Contents

Salutations and Signatures 92
Endings—and Beginnings 97
She also Serves who Only Stands and Waits 105
Always Leave them Laughing 110
Wear it Well 121

"HOW YA DOIN', DOC?" 125

Irvin 127
Partners 135
Teamwork 141
Eh-Heh-Heh-Heh-Chhemm! 144
Surprise! 151
It's a Boy! 163
Turn, Turn, Turn 170
The Last Valentine 179

"DA HELL MIT!" 185

Der Schlechter 187
If You Can't Beat 'em, Outsmart 'em! 196
The Driving Lesson 201
The Lion and the Mouse 209
Redemption 213

Bashert iz Bashert! 217

We Remember Them 223

Author's Foreward

Thomas Wolfe was wrong. You can go home again—if you hold on to your memories.

The people in these stories—Aunt Sophia, Uncle Irvin, Bubby and Zady—were strong personalities who had a powerful impact on me and on the rest of the family. I saw them everyday for the first nine years of my life. They were part of the air I breathed.

We referred to them as *The Family* to distinguish them from the rest of us. They were warm, nurturing, generous, funny, neurotic and eccentric, and I adored them. They loved me unconditionally.

Everyone should be born with a guarantee of unconditional love. It should be one of our inalienable rights, like life, liberty and the pursuit of happiness.

Each one of them lived such a long time, I thought I could keep them forever. Of course, I was wrong. Zady went first, then Bubby, then Uncle Irvin. Only Aunt Sophia remained, persistent and unyielding, sole bearer of the Family Flame. Finally, three years ago, it was her turn. Her death took me by surprise. I was not prepared to lose her.

Suddenly, I had a ragged, gaping hole inside of me that echoed with hollowness and ached with pain. She had been my spiritual anchor, and I hadn't even realized it. Without her I felt lost—abandoned. How could I let her go without losing myself along with her?

As the pain of her loss welled up within me, I began to write—first with outrage and indignation. Then finally, the nourishing feelings began to flow.

Author's Foreward

Aunt Sophia sprang to life on the paper, eagerly summoning Bubby, Uncle Irvin and Zady to join her. As usual, she took over—laughing, joking, prodding me with memories faster than I could get them down. Little by little, the jagged hole began to fill with warmth, love, and laughter. My appetite improved. I literally grew fat on the memories. Not only in body, but in spirit as well.

I embarked on a journey to my own land of Oz, and—like Dorothy—discovered that what I went looking for was deep inside me all the time.

December 18, 1991

Setting the Scene

It was my imminent birth which precipitated my parents' move from Oakley Avenue in 1938. They and my older sister Gischa had been living upstairs from Bubby and Zady (my maternal grandparents) and Aunt Sophia (my mother's older sister) for two years.

My mother felt suffocated by the cramped living space and the *constant* proximity of The Family. My expected arrival provided her with a convenient excuse for escape.

In a desperate bid for independence, my parents borrowed money and bought their first home—a block and a half up the street. Bubby could see our house from her front porch, yet she viewed our departure as a defection, and a personal affront. In retaliation, she refused to speak to my mother for several weeks.

When I finally arrived, a month later than expected, Bubby called a truce. She wanted to see her grandchildren. She forgave—but she didn't forget. She merely added this current "sin" to her already lengthy list. In Bubby's opinion, my mother had been comitting sins against her all her life.

My mother soon discovered that her quest for freedom had been in vain. The Family treated our house as if it were an annex to theirs. Bubby and Aunt Sophia visited daily.

Two years later, Uncle Irvin joined The Family, but instead of Aunt Sophia moving out, *he* moved in. "Married, shmarried," Aunt Sophia would shrug, what did that have to do with leaving Bubby?

Setting the Scene

Aunt Sophia and Uncle Irvin set up housekeeping in the apartment my parents had previously vacated, upstairs from Bubby and Zady. Now there were three people making the daily pilgrimage to our house. Zady was still working; he only came on special occasions.

Every evening after work, they "rushed" over so they could "see the children," before my mother, "The General," put us to bed. If one of us got sick, the number of visits increased in direct proportion to the seriousness of the illness. Bubby steamed back and forth with tasty morsels from her kitchen, hoping to tempt the sick child back to health. Aunt Sophia called from work several times a day. "Is she running a temperature? Did you call the doctor? What did he say?" Sometimes she'd ask to speak to the "patient." "Hi, honey, how are you feeling? What would you like me to bring you?"

Despite her daily visits, Bubby still expected my mother to call every morning with an up-to-the-minute bulletin on the state of our health—even when we were well! I'm sure she expected the same from Uncle Morris, my mother's younger brother, who lived two doors down with his family.

Of the five children Bubby had borne: Sophia, Joe, Mary, Morris and Harry, three lived near by. Joe, the first child born in this country, and the uncle for whom I am named, died in 1934. He was only twenty-seven. Harry, her "baby," eloped when he was twenty, and moved to Philadelphia.

She mourned the loss of them both.

From early childhood, I was aware of the impact The Family had on our lives. To me, they were benevolent fairy godparents who would grant my every wish. To my mother, they were the Four Horsemen of the Apocalypse, thundering down on her at every turn.

As giving and loving as they were to me, that's how exacting and demanding they were to my mother. Because I could empathize with her feelings of anger, pain, and helplessness, the pleasure I took in their company was always tempered by guilt. I felt like a piece of salt water taffy, being pulled in two directions at once.

Now that The Family is gone, I am free to embrace them without feeling disloyal to my mother, who is still alive. These stories are my tribute to them, the Guardians of my childhood, Champions of my right to laugh, cry, dream, and believe in Magic.

This is a celebration of their lives—now that I have finally learned to celebrate my own.

"Vey iz Mir!"

Sarah

Sarah was barely out of her teens when she was given, quite literally, in marriage to a stranger. That was the custom among Eastern European Jews at the turn of the century.

She was a timid girl, unschooled, unskilled and, she thought, unattractive. The world outside her small village frightened her. She only felt safe with her mother, Mimeh, and her sisters Channah and Ruchel Dvera.

Compared to her father, Aaron, who was very gentle, her new husband seemed harsh and tyrannical. He took her away from Berezne to his own town, Karpilifka, where she was the stranger. One day she had been a girl, the next she was a wife. Nine months later she gave birth to a baby girl she named Sophia. Now she was also expected to be a mother!

Sarah was used to working beside her mother and her sisters. She yearned to return to her girlhood; she missed daily life on the farm. Michael made her nervous with his hollering. She couldn't seem to please him, no matter how hard she tried. All right, so he was a hard worker. But would it have killed him, *Nishtu gedacht,* to be a little kind?

Then without warning, a terrible thing happened. She was waiting to serve him supper, but he didn't come home. Days passed with no sign or word from him. What could have happened? Was he dead? Pooh, pooh, pooh! Had she and Sophia been abandoned?

Sarah

Sarah was alone with her baby when the military police stormed in. Where was her husband, Michael? they demanded. Paralyzed with terror, she swore she didn't know. Rampaging through the house like wounded animals, they destroyed everything they touched.

As soon as they left, she grabbed Sophia and ran to a neighbor who hid her until nightfall. Under cover of darkness, crouched in the back of a wagon, she and little Sophia were smuggled to the edge of the forest that separated Sarah from her mother's farm.

All night Sarah ran through the woods, clutching her infant against her. Suppose she were caught and punished— or eaten by wild animals? She literally ran for her life.

Someone must have been watching over her. By the next morning, she was home. Baruch Hashem! But where was Michael? Alive? Or dead.

Months passed. She was back in the familiar routine. As long as she stayed under Mimeh's roof, she was safe.

Then a letter arrived from Michael, from Baltimore, U.S.A! He had been seized on the street, and conscripted into the Russian army, but he and another man had escaped. He was living with her brother, Morris, working as a presser in a garment factory. The pay was low and the hours were long, but he was saving money for her ticket. Then, he would send for her.

Sarah was terrified. America! An ocean away! She didn't want to go to America. She pushed it out of her mind and immersed herself in the life of her family, helping her mother on the farm, and taking care of her precious Sophia. For eighteen months, her life continued uninterrupted.

Then, one terrrible day, her ticket came. She had to leave her mother. It was like cutting out her own heart.

Mimeh loaded her down with dishes, linens, feather beds, heavy brass candlesticks for the Sabbath, a large brass samovar—all the things she thought her daughter would need in such a distant, God-forsaken land.

Sarah tore herself away from the love and security of her family. She knew she would never see any of them again.

A friend of her father's smuggled her into Germany. When she got to Bremen, exhausted, hungry, filthy, and bereft, she was herded onto the steamship Neckar, with hundreds of other emigrating Jews.

Behind her was everything she knew and, except for Sophia, everything she cared for. Ahead lay who knew what? Reunion with a man she didn't know, or even like? A new country where everything would be strange--including the language? *Vey iz mir!* How would she manage? Who would take care of her?

The voyage was even worse than she expected. For three weeks, she was jammed together with hundreds of men, women, and children in the bottom of a boat. Ventilation was poor. Sanitation was primitive. The stench was constant and suffocating. She, and most of the others, were sick the whole time. If it hadn't been for Sophia, she would have asked God to let her die.

Sophia was all she had left, a living remnant of the beloved life she was leaving forever. Sarah clung as tenaciously to Sophia as a child clings to her security blanket. Sophia, sensing her mother's dependence on her, clung back. Together they entered America to begin their new life.

In time, most children outgrow their need for security blankets. For Sarah and Sophia, that time would never come.

Sarah was my grandmother, my Bubby, and this was her initiation into adulthood. Her life never got any better. There was too much loss. In 1934, her son Joe died. He had been her first boy, and the hope of the family. That wound never healed.

Sarah

It wasn't until the late 1940's when the war was over, that Sarah received news of her family in Russia. Her mother had starved to death. Her sisters, their husbands and children, had been brutally murdered by Nazis. Her grief overwhelmed her.

She always said that when she came to this country she cried for six months. She mourned for the rest of her life.

Bubby was the storyteller in our family. Now I continue her tradition. Although she died twenty-one years ago, I can feel her gentle presence *alive* within me. We share so many things, a sense of humor, an understanding of human nature and a deep and abiding love of children. How often she rises unbidden in my mind and heart.

"Jo-Vennala," she murmurs shyly, plucking at the edges of my consciousness, "Jo-vennala, I vant to tell you someting." She smiles her sweet patient smile, and waits for me to listen.

Bubby and the Butcher

In my neighborhood we had two kosher butchers—one named Kostinsky and one named Surosky, but Bubby called them both by the same name. "*Di Choleria.*"

Choleria means cholera. She believed that these butchers were cheating her. This hard-working, illiterate immigrant had raised five hungry children. Money was scarce. By overcharging her, these men had literally taken food out of the mouths of her children. To Bubby's way of thinking, this was an unforgivable sin. Therefore, they deserved one of her most pungent and colorful Yiddish curses—to be called by the name of a dreaded disease.

According to my grandmother, a Jew who cheated a fellow Jew was a *goniff*. Such a terrible creature was beneath her contempt. Her justice, like that of her God's, was swift and merciless. Outraged by her own sense of powerlessness, she unleashed the only weapon she had, her sharp tongue. She wielded her tongue the way the butchers wielded their cleavers, with deadly accuracy. One deft thrust, and she had sliced away their humanity. They were no longer individuals. They were symbols of destruction, like the cholera for which they were now named.

In addition, she used the plural construction "*di*," thereby extending the curse to *all* kosher butchers on both sides of the Atlantic—those who had once been butchers, those who were currently butchers, and those unborn butchers yet to come.

Whenever Bubby had been "by *di choleria*," she came home with a face "*like a thirty-day rain.*" The best chicken had been sold to the lady in front of her. To her, he had sold garbage—and over-charged her besides!

Her mutterings and imprecations provided a musical counterpoint to the bangings and slammings of her dinner preparations. *The chicken would be tough. The whole meal would be a disaster!* But she was wrong. The chicken was delicious—so tender and succulent—the meat fell right off the bone.

My mouth still waters for her Sabbath roasted chicken. I have never yet tasted its equal. I'm sure I never will.

Bubby and the Birthday Cake

My Bubby was a wonderful cook, and an intuitive one. She couldn't read, so she cooked by instinct. Whatever she made came out of her head and heart. Her sponge cake was my favorite. It was not to be believed. She did all the beating by hand and she whipped the batter with such ferocious intensity that huge pockets of air were absorbed. As the cake baked, it rose higher and higher until at last it emerged—a golden brown pillar of perfection.

The top was the best part. It was paler in color and covered with a delicate network of tiny openings that glistened with moisture. I couldn't resist touching that soft, smooth surface. It felt sticky, and wherever my finger exerted the slightest pressure, it bounced.

I adored those cakes. Not only because they were delicious, but because Bubby put so much of herself into them. Every year on my birthday, she made one especially for me, and every year she created a masterpiece.

Like many things in Bubby's life, my birthday sponge cake became a Family ritual. Since we reprised it every year, remembering our parts wasn't difficult

The date is May 23. The evening is warm and balmy. Dinner is over, but it's still light outside. From the front porch, I can watch the procession as it wends its disparate way up our street. Bubby is in the lead, her square diminutive body wrapped in a shapeless pink house dress. Black orthopedic shoes crack and bulge around her bunioned feet. Eyes straight ahead, lips clamped together, she strides

Bubby and the Birthday Cake

purposefully toward me, bearing before her The Annual Birthday Offering.

Half a block behind Bubby trips Aunt Sophia. "Don't rush, you'll live longer" is her battle cry. She propels her tightly corseted body forward one zoftig foot at a time. When she gets closer, I will hear her stockings whisper. Plump pink toes, their nails brightly polished, peek seductively through the openings of her dainty high-heeled shoes. As the distance lengthens between them, Aunt Sophia calls out to Bubby. "Ma. Where are you running? Ma!"

Wordlessly, Bubby marches on, her face solemn.

Sauntering a few paces behind Aunt Sophia, is Uncle Irvin. He rocks on the balls of his feet as he walks, as if he were bouncing on a trampoline. His dark hair is slicked back and still damp from his shower.

At the end of the line is my Zady. His voluminous seersucker pants strain at his ample middle, then billow around his stumpy limbs like sails. Leaning forward, he thunks his heavy cane against the sidewalk, dragging his withered leg.

Bubby arrives first, and hands me a plate covered with a clean white dish towel. "It no be's good," she assures me, her eyes filling with tears. She is absolutely convinced the cake is a failure. With humble apology, she removes the snowy covering. Behold! The cake is exposed in all its luscious splendor. It is a miracle! It is a work of art! Everyone oohs and aahs, but Bubby will not be comforted.

We light the candles and sing *Happy Birthday*. Mother slices the cake, and Daddy tops each piece with a square of harlequin ice cream. Everyone digs in.

"Delicious, delicious," we murmur through bulging mouthfulls. The cake, as always, is a sensation. Bubby hovers in the background shaking her palsied head. She refuses even to taste it. Mournfully she intones, "A myby next year it be better."

Bubby Battles the Bulge

Bubby not only had a terrible sense of inferiority. She was also an implacable perfectionist. Needless to say, this combination of traits did not make her life any easier. Although she spoke Russian, Polish and Yiddish fluently, her command of English was severely limited, and so embarrassed her that she refused to attend night school with the other immigrants. She was sure that her accent was far worse than any of theirs. As a result, her vocabulary was both creative and unusual—to say the least!

The word *maybe* she pronounced *a myby*. Rice Krispies became *Krice Krispies*. Her tightly-curled hair-do she referred to as a *pear-manint*. The cleaning woman, whose name was Marcella, had to answer instead to *Costello*. Uncle Irvin used to say "Bubby doesn't fracture the English language, she pulverizes it!"

Her original pronunciations invariably caught us unaware, and we'd explode into gales of helpless laughter. Bubby watched us shyly; then she laughed too. She didn't seem to mind being the object of our hilarity.

Besides perceiving herself as the most ignorant creature on Earth, Bubby was also convinced she was the ugliest. Scrutiny made her nervous. If, in her judgment, I looked at her a moment longer than she deemed necessary, she'd smile beseechingly at me and ask, "Vy you look auf me, Jo-vennala? I'm an ugly poyson." And nothing I said could dissuade her.

Because she was short—maybe 4'-11" and squarish—her body appeared heavy. But she only weighed one hundred and thirty-three pounds. She always weighed one hundred and thirty-three pounds. It never varied. I know because it was my job to weigh her—from the time I learned to read numbers until the day I got married.

Every Sunday night, we re-enacted the same ritual. For a short time after she arrived, Bubby sat quietly pretending to be invisible. Meanwhile the rest of the family talked and argued. Since Bubby was too deaf to hear the "discussions," she simply watched our facial expressions and gyrations, enjoying all the tumult. Her eyes sparkled with merriment as my father and Uncle Irvin expressed their differing political views simultaneously, their bodies tense, their arms stabbing the air with exasperation. She said we were funnier than *I Love Lucy*.

After about half-an-hour she would rise, pad over and motion for me to follow. She led me across the living room, up the stairway, and straight into the bathroom. Mutely, she'd point to the scale. Bending forward, I'd pull it into the middle of the room for her, then wait while she prepared herself to ascend.

Arranging her features in a wry expression, she'd poke at her middle, then pinch the excess flesh on her sides. "Fat!" she'd exclaim, curling her lip in self-derision. That was my cue. "Bubby, you're not fat!" I'd respond. She'd flash me a look that said: it's not nice to fool an old lady. Then, like Jean d'Arc, she'd steel herself for battle and hop on the scale.

With chin lifted and eyes straight ahead, Bubby waited gravely for me to pass sentence. She was certain she had gained at least fifty pounds since the previous Sunday. Her face shone with the light of exquisite martyrdom.

I squinted down at the tiny numbers. "It's one hundred and thirty-three, Bubby—just like last week."

Bubby bestowed on me a look of perfect incredulity. Then she smiled sadly and shook her head. "You make fun auf me," she crooned.

"Bubby, I swear! It's one hundred and thirty-three. You're not fat!"

Had she known Latin, she would probably have said "*Et tu, Brute*." As it was, she merely dismissed me with a resigned flick of her wrist, and returned to the family in the living room. The following Sunday we repeated the entire performance, word for word, and gesture for gesture.

Bubby Goes by Johnson's

In some families, eating out is a common-place activity. They select a restaurant, order dinner, eat, and leave. Not in my Family. Like everything else in their lives, eating out required a special ritual. A new restaurant must be broken in. Only then was it added to The Family's repertoire. Once adopted, that restaurant became their refuge, their sanctuary.

But the first visit—like a first kiss—was crucial, and could be filled with drama. Like the first time they went "by Johnson's," as Bubby came to call it. Howard Johnson's to you and me.

Picture the cozy interior of an ordinary restaurant on a cold winter's evening. Bubby bobs through the revolving door followed by Aunt Sophia, then Uncle Irvin. They are welcomed by the unsuspecting hostess.

"Four," Aunt Sophia replies in response to the hostess' question. Although Zady is not yet in evidence, she expects him momentarily—the way Bubby expects the *mashiach*. Aunt Sophia can't begin to guess what's keeping the *mashiach*, but she knows that Zady will appear as soon as he can extricate himself from the back seat of the car.

The hostess leads them to a table, expecting them to sit no doubt. Instead, Bubby stops in the middle of the aisle, mute and motionless, and remains there as if she had turned to stone. Meanwhile Aunt Sophia, clutching her black leather pocket book, and the brown paper sack she is never without, wanders around and around the table. The fine white fur on her collar wafts gently in her wake.

Uncle Irvin stops, lights a cigarette, and props his elbow against the top of a nearby booth, turning the full force of his baby blue eyes upon his hostess.

"How're you-all *doin'* this evening?" he inquires affably. Uncle Irvin has nothing but time.

Aunt Sophia comes to roost after successfully completing several circuits. With obvious reluctance she places her parcels on the nearest chair. First she puts the purse down in front of the sack. Then she moves the sack around in front of the purse. She stands for a moment surveying her handiwork. Satisfied, she bustles over to Bubby.

Bubby waits, still frozen in time as Aunt Sophia lifts the purse from her arm, and adds it to her recently assembled still life. Now there are two bags and a sack. There is a slight pause while Aunt Sophia recovers the symmetry of her arrangement. Then she removes Bubby's coat, gives it a vigorous shake, and waggles it at Uncle Irvin.

Although his eyes never leave the eyes of his hostess, Uncle Irvin snaps to attention. Leaning toward Aunt Sophia, he scoops up the coat, and folds it neatly across his blue-jacketed arm. Mission accomplished, he lounges back, and continues to *kibbitz* with the busy hostess.

Bubby's nylon scarf has slipped down over her shoulders. Aunt Sophia *schleps* it back around her neck, patting and smoothing it into place. Rummaging in the sack, she produces Bubby's thick pink cardigan, and bundles Bubby into it.

"Here, Ma," Aunt Sophia bellows, extending a chair toward Bubby. Bubby comes to life briefly, takes the proffered chair—and sits.

This is Uncle Irvin's cue. Without losing a beat in the conversation, he undrapes his burly body from the booth, steps behind Aunt Sophia, and peels her coat from her ample shoulders. Laying Aunt Sophia's coat on top of Bubby's, he sashays forward, and gallantly pulls out her chair. "Enjoy!" gasps the hostess, and streaks back to the milling throng. Uncle Irvin stashes the haberdashery, and takes his seat next to Aunt Sophia.

The waitress, who has been watching from the sidelines, darts over, and swishes a soggy grey *shmata* across the once white formica. Crumbs spray in every direction. She plunks scalloped paper placemats down on the still moist table, adds napkins, "silverware," and water, and confidently hands out menus. Sliding her order pad out of her pocket, she waits, pencil poised.

By now Zady has successfully negotiated the treacheries of the revolving door, and is limping down the aisle toward them. Thunk. Step, slide. Thunk. Step, slide. Finally, he reaches the table. Hooking his cane onto the edge for balance he wedges his cumbersome body into the remaining chair. Aunt Sophia and Uncle Irvin pore over their menus.

Bubby makes a *zoer* face.

Aunt Sophia: **"What's the matter, Ma?"** When it comes to her mother, no nuance, no matter how infinitesimal, escapes Aunt Sophia's ever-present antennae.

Bubby explains in Yiddish that she feels a draft.

Aunt Sophia puts down her menu and rises with grave dignity. Gathering up their parcels, she heads for another table. Bubby hops off her chair and trots meekly after. Uncle Irvin retrieves the coats, and ambles after Bubby. Zady sighs, then reaches a claw-like hand toward his cane.

Aunt Sophia settles Bubby at a new location. The frazzled waitress, who has followed faithfully in their footsteps, springs forward and swipes at the new table. Having learned nothing from the last few minutes, she redistributes the menus.

Meanwhile, back at the first table, Zady hoists himself to his feet. As Aunt Sophia and Uncle Irvin resume reading, Zady begins his second perilous journey toward them.

Bubby waits until Zady, puffing from exertion, is again seated. Then she makes another face.

"Ma! Vus a de mer?"

Wordlessly, Bubby indicates the heat vent. Everyone gets up and moves to another table.

Bubby knows exactly what she is looking for. She wants a table that allows her to people-watch in any direction, is convenient to the bathroom without being too close, and is far from the noise and bustle of the kitchen, yet close enough for the food to arrive hot. By the time she finds even a close approximation, Zady is exhausted, and the poor waitress is frantic!

That was the beginning of the Family's long sojourn at Johnson's. From that day on, that table became "their" table, and that's where they ate their dinner for the next ten years. At first they only went on Sundays. Then Bubby developed heart trouble and Parkinson's, and she was forbidden to cook or clean anymore.

Around the same time, Aunt Sophia developed an eye problem which forced her to retire early from her secretarial job. For the first time since high school, she was home every day. Unfortunately, so was Zady. He was angry at her for sabotaging his cleaning business. She was angry at him for tyrannizing Bubby.

The cold war which had simmered between them for years, finally came to the boil. Minor scuffles escalated into major assaults. The atmosphere fairly twanged with tension. Bubby's head and arm shook uncontrollably, and it wasn't only from the Parkinson's! Aunt Sophia decided to remove Bubby from the front lines.

And that's how the new ritual was inaugurated. Every day at two o'clock, as soon as she had completed her toilette, Aunt Sophia took Bubby and ran away from Zady.

Bubby goes by Johnson's

They spent their days doing errands and visiting doctors, timing their arrival "by Johnson's" for precisely six o'clock. The entire staff turned out to greet them.

By the time Uncle Irvin finished work and joined them, Bubby and Aunt Sophia had culled all the gossip. They hastened to enlighten him about Stella's sick baby or Jimmy's incarcerated brother-in-law. Uncle Irvin listened to each tale of woe, and commiserated with each heartbroken victim. Then he and Aunt Sophia fanned out to include the other diners. Only after they had exchanged warm greetings with the regulars, and graciously welcomed the newcomers were they finally ready for dinner—the main event.

Here is the scene as it played nightly. In all those years, only the waitresses changed—never the dialogue.

Aunt Sophia to waitress: "What's your name, honey?"
Waitress: "Virginia."
Aunt Sophia (confidentially) to waitress: "What's good, tonight, honey?"

Her tone implies, "It's all right. You can trust me."
Waitress: "The fish is nice."
Aunt Sophia: "Is it fresh?"

The waitress swears on her mother's grave that the fish is fresh. Aunt Sophia apprises Bubby of the waitress's suggestion, shouting to overcome Bubby's hearing loss. Bubby considers, then shakes her head.

Aunt Sophia: "What else, honey? What else is good?"

The waitress makes several more suggestions, each with an assurance of freshness. Bubby refuses each one. Nothing sounds good to her. They have reached an impasse.

Aunt Sophia : "Look at her, poor thing. She eats like a bird."

She ticks off each of Bubby's medical problems and explains how they affect both her appetite and her digestion in minute detail.

Finally, Aunt Sophia places Bubby's fate squarely in the hands of the waitress.

Aunt Sophia (in a beseeching tone): "What do *you* think she should have, Virginia?"

The waitress seems flattered, and rises to the occasion.

Waitress: "How about a nice piece of fish?"

Aunt Sophia (bellows in Yiddish): **"Virginia says you should have a nice piece of fish, Ma."**

Bubby weighs Virginia's suggestion, then shrugs and nods acquiescence.

Aunt Sophia: "You don't think it will hurt her, huh? Poor thing. She's not well."

Virginia again assures Aunt Sophia that Bubby will be all right with the fish. Aunt Sophia orders the fish for Bubby. One down—two to go.

Now Virginia has to go through the whole thing again while Aunt Sophia and Uncle Irvin make their choices. After fifteen minutes, Virginia finally has all three orders. Having assured and reassured Aunt Sophia as to the quality of the food and the wisdom of her choices, she heads toward the kitchen.

Aunt Sophia (shouting loud enough for the whole restaurant to hear): **"Virginia, Virginia."**

Waitress: "Ma'am?"

Aunt Sophia: **"Make sure it's fresh!"**

After a big dinner, including ice cream parfaits for dessert, Aunt Sophia and Uncle Irvin become expansive. Out come the pictures of the nieces and nephews, the grand-nieces and grand-nephews. They regale the attentive staff with stories about their precocious progeny. *We* have become the children they never had. The Family *shmoozes* for the rest of the evening. They rarely leave before ten o' clock.

Although I knew that Johnson's was a regular part of The Family's life, I didn't understand its true significance until many years later. My husband, my two daughters and I were living in Rochester, New York. I had flown back to

Baltimore on one of my infrequent visits. Nothing would do, but that I *must* go with them "by Johnson's." They wanted to offer me some hospitality in their "home" away from home.

When we walked in the door, there was a quickening, a sense of excitement. Several members of the staff materialized around us. They took turns embracing Bubby.

"Look who's here; look who's here," I heard as busboys and waitresses appeared from every side. Aunt Sophia beamed and greeted everyone as if she were the Queen of Albania. With graceful majesty, she introduced each server, bestowing praise and encouragement upon all.

"And this is Edna, honey. She works hard and takes good care of us, even though I'm *afraid* we're a lot of trouble." She was indicating a tall thin woman on my left. Edna, picking up on Aunt Sophia's signal, immediately denied that they were anything but a pleasure to serve.

"Edna's a widow, honey. Her husband had a bad heart. She's had a lot of trouble in her life."

Aunt Sophia turned to Edna. "You're a good person, Edna, and a good waitress." She patted Edna's arm. Edna smiled and blushed, then turned to Bubby.

"And how's our little Mother today?" she cooed, putting her arm around Bubby's shoulder.

Bubby started explaining in Yiddish how she was. Her voice quavered with emotion as she described some of the sadder moments of her life beginning with her marriage to Zady, and touching on her arrival in steerage to this country in 1906. Aunt Sophia provided a simultaneous translation, like in the United Nations.

Edna, listening sympathetically, patted Bubby's arm and crooned over her the way a mother croons to a child in need of comfort. I just stood there feeling dazed.

When Bubby finished speaking, Aunt Sophia drew Edna's attention to me. "And this is my niece Jo-Ann!"

Edna's face lit up. "Oh, you're the one from *Rochester*! How are Missy and Sharon? How's Stanley?"

Gathering momentum, she peppered me with questions. "Are the children over their strep throats yet? How are Sharon's tonsils? Did Missy do well in the play?"

I stared at the woman in amazement. Then I looked at Aunt Sophia. She began to laugh, nervously. She knew she had crossed a line with me.

"Don't be mad, honey, don't be mad. I read Edna your letters and showed her all the pictures you sent. It's O.K., Edna's like family."

With great difficulty I remembered the manners my parents had taught me. Then I remembered how very much I adored Aunt Sophia. I managed to answer Edna's questions and even thanked her for her interest.

Edna lovingly removed Bubby's coat and seated her with the deference one reserves for The Queen Mother. I watched my grandmother expand with pleasure.

What else, I wondered, did this woman know about my personal life? I tried to recall the things I had written to Aunt Sophia. Whatever private thoughts I had shared were no longer private. I realized that in future letters, when I began, "Dear Aunt Sophia," I would mentally have to add, "and Edna."

Bubby Buys a Chair

When bad things happened in other people's families, Bubby sympathized. But when bad things happened in her family, she bowed her head. *"Ich hub nit kane mazel,"* she explained. What she really meant was, *"isn't that just my luck?"*

When Joe died, she blamed herself. Maybe if she'd been a better mother? And her family, murdered in the Holocaust, if she'd been a better daughter? Sister? Couldn't she have saved *them*?

Bubby believed that *HASHEM* was punishing her. Therefore, she had accepted His "punishments," no matter how painful, as her due. Finally, when *her* health broke down, she rebelled. This time God had gone too far! He had taken her sense of purpose. The only thing of value she had left.

Bubby stalked through the house, jaw clenched, hands fisted. "Doctors, shmoctors," she raged. "What do they know? They give you pills, and the pills make you sicker!" She clamped her lips together, and refused all medication.

Aunt Sophia coaxed, threatened and begged, but for once Bubby's deafness worked to her advantage. She ignored Aunt Sophia's pleadings—not to mention the doctor's orders—and resumed cooking and taking care of the house. She'd show them! Behind Aunt Sophia's back, she threw the hated prescriptions in the garbage.

But fury alone could not sustain her. She was too weak, and too sick. Once again she was forced to stop. What could she do, rail against God? *Nishtu Gedach!* What terrible calamity might that bring? All the energy she'd previously expended for survival, she now channelled into grief. She became morose and withdrawn, mourning all the ungrieved losses of her life.

Her suffering was palpable. She carried it before her, like a banner, hugging it to her bosom, as she would hug a loved child. She swaddled herself in its thick folds, insulating herself against the world.

Her diminutive body took up so little space in the universe, yet she endeavored to take even less. Bubby gave new meaning to the word self-effacing. She could blend into backgrounds like a chameleon, or—while she was sitting right next to you—she could disappear at will. She never vacated a chair, without erasing the imprint she'd left on it—as if she had never sat there at all.

Her large solemn eyes peered sadly through square rimless spectacles. *I have served long and hard, at great cost, but I expect nothing in return,* they seemed to say. Her tightly-coiffed head shook uncontrollably. Her right arm, flaccid now with disuse, trembled at her side. It hurt just to look at her.

That's when they started going by Johnson's every night. The waitresses and customers adopted Bubby, encouraging her to talk. It was just what she needed. Between her penchant for melodrama, and her ability to touch people's hearts, she captivated them. She thrived on the attention and the nurturing. At home, she might feel invisible, but by Johnson's, she was *somebody!*

After awhile Bubby spent so much time sitting by Johnson's every day, she developed an attachment to her chair. She confided to Aunt Sophia that this chair was *"azay git."* Whenever she lowered herself onto it, she heaved a deep and satisfied sigh. *"Ahhhh, a mechiah!"* In time, her budding appreciation flowered. Johnson's chair became the best she had ever sat on. Finally, she declared it the only chair on which she could ever again be comfortable—in this life—or the next.

I heard about the chair the next time I came into Baltimore. It contrasted so sharply with the rest of Bubby's furniture, I noticed it the minute I walked into the breakfast room.

"What's this?" I asked Aunt Sophia, pointing to the pale diminutive shape.

"Oh, that's Bubby's chair. From Johnson's," she explained.

"You bought a chair from Howard Johnson's?"

If it was hard for the rest of us to deny Bubby anything, for Aunt Sophia it was almost impossible.

"Bubby said it was the only chair she could sit on."

"Does she sit on it?"

Aunt Sophia laughed. "Bubby says 'It isn't good here. It's only good by Johnson's.'"

Aunt Sophia kept the chair, even though it failed to live up to its promise. She took it with them when they sold the house and moved to a small apartment. It remained there for years, forgotten in a corner. Every time I saw it I thought of Bubby. What a symbol that chair must have been for her—a constant reminder of how powerless she really was—in a dangerous, unpredictable, and incomprehensible world.

Bubby and Ma Bell

Bubby didn't make her dive into the murky waters of the Twentieth Century till she was well into her forties. And then she was pushed. The year was 1923, and Zady had just purchased a house with central heating and indoor plumbing. Then, on top of everything else, he ordered a telephone!

With the heating and plumbing, Bubby managed a peaceful coexistence. They were self-maintaining, and rarely needed her intervention. But the telephone was a different story. With that, she had to interact!

As a devoutly superstitious person, Bubby harbored a deep-seated suspicion of anything mechanical. Her hands she knew she could count on, but a machine? That talks to you yet? *"Vey iz mir!"*

Since the new house was out in *"alleh drerden,"* as Bubby put it, she would have no neighbors. How would she manage if she needed something? Even in the Old Country, she had always been able to summon help on foot. With five children she was afraid to be so isolated. That would be too much temptation for the Evil Eye!

Because her fear for her children outweighed her inhibitions, Bubby tolerated the new contraption. But she avoided it the way a timid child avoids a dark closet. *Michel* was the breadwinner; let him take care of it! She was only related to the telephone by marriage.

Bubby's knowlege of science was as meager as her distrust of mechanical objects was great. She couldn't figure out how the voices got through those skinny wires. When her children explained that sound travels through the air, Bubby said:

"You talk to the air and it comes here? Such a country, America!" She shook her head in wonderous disbelief.

But it wasn't only her ignorance of science that made her uncomfortable. As she would have put it, she had "plenny" other reasons besides that! For one thing, she was beginning to lose her hearing. For another, she had never learned to read or write. Understanding the operator was difficult for her. Getting the operator to understand her was nearly impossible.

Years went by. With a husband and five children in the house, Bubby found she could avoid Ma Bell, and Ma Bell, *denks gott,* returned the favor. Then everything changed. Without even asking her permission, Bubby's children grew up. Worse than that, they got married and moved out! All except Sophia, her oldest.

Bubby was in a quandry. How could she continue to keep an eye on her baby birds, when they were no longer living in the nest? Remaining involved with her offspring was crucial. Otherwise, how could she tell them the right things to do? Suddenly she could see the possibilities in her old nemesis. Her phone line stretched like an extended umbilical cord into the homes of her children. It could even reach Harry's in Philadelphia. Bubby learned to manipulate that phone with the virtuosity of a Toscanini, orchestrating the dynamic of the whole family with one flick of her diminutive wrist. In her own way, she had always been a master of communication. Now with the help of Ma Bell, she became an Ph. D.

How well I remember the daily ritual. After she got Daddy off for work, and my sister, Gischa off to school, Mother would dial the fated number. Liberty 9174. By the time I was three, I knew her opening words by heart.

Mother: "Hello Ma."

Pause for Bubby's answer.

Mother: *"Ibn alright, vus machts-di?"*

Mother's voice barely concealed the irritation she felt over these required expressions of filial obedience, but for her rebellion would have been out of the question. She had learned years ago that rebellion only begot recrimination, and recrimination always begot guilt.

She would eventually have to resume the calls anyway, bearing the additional burden of Transgressor. As a Transgressor she would have to prove her worthiness before being reinstated into Bubby's good graces. Since this process could take some time, Mother decided it was easier just to call.

With her children, Bubby spoke Yiddish, but to her grandchildren she had to speak "Ang-lish" which for her was more like ang-*uish!*

If she called and I answered, she would quaver, "Jo-Vennala, get Maadder." (Mother) Then she refused to speak another word until "Maadder" came on the line.

If I called there and *she* answered, I would hear a faint "Ha-looooh?" She always stretched the single word into at least five syllables.

"It's Jo-Ann, Bubby."

"Vait a minute." There would be a long silence while she went to find Sophia or Irvin.

In later years, when her hearing became too impaired, she recruited Aunt Sophia to place her calls. Mother would pick up the phone and hear Aunt Sophia's funereal announcement: "Mary? Mommy has something to tell you."

Uh-oh. Bubby was going to make a speech. *That* meant trouble.

Mother's already pale face blanched. Foreboding filled the room. What dastardly deed had she committed this time? Whatever it was, retribution was imminent. Mother clenched her teeth. Her fingers tightened perceptibly around the receiver.

"Hello Ma." Mother sounded reluctant, but resolute, like a prisoner awaiting the firing squad.

"Mare'n?" quavered Bubby at her most pathetic. Then she'd deliver the Yiddish equivalent of "You should live with your family and be well, till a hundred and twenty years, and never darken my door again."

Slam! went the phone. Mother would just stand there, stunned and blinking as if a balloon had suddenly exploded in her face. Bubby had given the umbilical cord a very effective yank!

Mother's crime was usually Not Asking Bubby's Advice. *This*, Bubby could not forgive. She expected to be consulted on everything. From how to cook a chicken, to what to name a baby. My mother, who never asked her advice, was *schlecht*. Aunt Sophia, who always asked her advice, was *git* .

Of course, once Bubby had given her advice, she expected us to take it. Anyone who didn't was considered misguided, and had to suffer the consequences. Like my sister, Gischa, and the episode of the highchair.

I was married and in my own home by this time. Aunt Sophia called.

"Hi, honey. How are you?"

"Fine, Aunt Sophia. How are you?"

" I'm afraid I'll live. Listen honey, I want you to talk to Gischa. Bubby says the reason that Cheri gets sick so much is because Gischa feeds her *in front of the refrigerator*. Every time Gischa opens the door—the child gets a draft. Bubby says it isn't good. *I* told Gischa, but she didn't listen. *You* tell her, honey, she's your sister. If *you* tell her—she'll listen."

The key words were "Bubby says." Whenever Aunt Sophia started a sentence like that, I knew better than to argue. Aunt Sophia regarded Bubby as a prophet and a sage. As Bubby's self-appointed disciple, she made it her mission to spread Bubby's Word. Missions were taken very seriously in my Family.

But even after *I* told her, the next time Bubby and Aunt Sophia came to visit Gischa, they found her feeding Cheri in front of the refrigerator. Aunt Sophia was forced to call in the reserves. Eventually, Gischa was so beseiged with calls from well-meaning relatives, she had to move the highchair—at least when Bubby and Aunt Sophia came to call.

They were like characters out of a 1940's detective movie. Bubby sat stoically in the background, like Sidney Greenstreet, and evoked a presence, while Aunt Sophia played the Peter Lorre role. Her job was to collect information to which Bubby listened carefully. There would be a short pause while Bubby considered all the alternatives. Only then, did she pronounce judgment.

With practice, Aunt Sophia and Bubby developed their two tiered telephone system into an Art. Then they took it on the road.

One Saturday afternoon, when I was visiting my sister, Aunt Sophia and Bubby stopped off on their way downtown. Before leaving Gischa's, Aunt Sophia decided to call some downtown theaters to see what was playing. Movies were a regular part of the downtown ritual. Each time a ticket lady answered, Aunt Sophia would say:

"Hello honey, could you kindly tell me what your feature presentation is today?"

Aunt Sophia would listen carefully, then pass the information on to her mother in Yiddish. We watched Bubby's face for some sign, but there was nothing. Aunt Sophia turned back to the ticket lady.

"Thank you, honey. Now could you please tell me who's in it?"

Again there was a pause. Then Aunt Sophia relayed this additional information to Bubby. Still no response. Aunt Sophia would thank the woman for her trouble and call the next theater.

One by one she went through all the theaters, except two. These happened to be across the street from each other. Aunt Sophia tried the first one. Not even a flicker of interest appeared on Bubby's solemn face when she heard the name of that picture. Ditto with the cast of characters, but Aunt Sophia was not discouraged. "Tell me honey, what's your name? Virginia? That's a pretty name! O.K. Virginia, look across the street, and tell me what's playing at the Stanley."

My sister began to squirm. In an unrealistic effort to quell what she regarded as an outrageous breach of ettiquette, she murmured, "Aunt Sophia ..." in a warning voice.

But Gisch should have known better. Stopping a runaway train would be easier!

Aunt Sophia waved Gischa aside and repeated to Bubby the name of the picture playing at the Stanley. No response from Bubby.

Aunt Sophia tried again.

"And tell me, Virginia, who's playing in *that* picture?"

Still no response from Bubby.

"If you would be so kind, Virginia," requested Aunt Sophia in her sweetest, most persuasive voice, "what is the picture about?"

"Aunt Sophia!" Gischa was beside herself. "You're not supposed to do that! Hang up. Hang up!" After all, it was *her* phone Aunt Sophia was using, and Gischa felt guilty by implication.

But Aunt Sophia could not be derailed. Ignoring Gischa's pleas, she turned to Bubby, and translated

Virginia's words into Yiddish. Everyone looked at Bubby. Virginia, the ticket lady, was still on the line.

With a perfectly blank face, Bubby sat thinking it over. Slowly her forehead began to pucker. Then the corners of her mouth turned down. She smacked the air with a curt dismissive gesture. *"Ah, hub zein in drerd!"* she proclaimed.

"Never mind, honey," Aunt Sophia said to the ticket lady, and hung up the phone. Why we had to go through all that I'll never know. Bubby always fell asleep as soon as the feature started.

The original candlestick phone that Zady leased in 1923 became a permanent member of their household. It remained on the little table in the vestibule for forty-four years. Nobody else had a phone like that. It was special, like The Family.

For me it became a symbol of them—of their incredible endurance in a rapidly changing world. They survived all the blows Fate dealt them: religious persecution, dire poverty, the loss of their country, their families, and the untimely death of a beloved brother and son. Around them swirled upheaval: economic depression, a world war, The Bomb. But, like the old telephone, they endured.

Who they were, how they behaved, the words they spoke, all remained the same. Within that house, time stood still for almost fifty years, and—like the eye of a hurricane—it was the safest place for a child to be.

Bubby at the Bradford

Some people panic when their lives feel overwhelming. Bubby and Aunt Sophia went downtown. Every Thursday and every Saturday, for years. Nothing interfered with this bi-weekly tradition—not war, not pestilence—not even a streetcar strike. They merely took a cab. Endlessly repeating certain rituals seemed to get them through the *mishegas* known as life.

For twenty years these trips followed a prescribed program. Since Aunt Sophia was never ready to leave before two p.m., and because she never undertook anything on an empty stomach, they always began with lunch.

On Thursdays, lunch would be followed by shopping, a visit to the hairdresser, a lavish and leisurely dinner, and a movie. Bubby enjoyed the color and liveliness of the MGM musicals, but a comedy or drama always put her to sleep. It was the best rest she got all week. Once Bubby drifted into dreamland, even the Three Stooges couldn't awaken her.

The Saturday schedule differed in one particular. Hairdressing was replaced by business administration. Aunt Sophia conducted all her business from her downtown office—the ladies' lounge in Hutzler's Department Store. Their management had graciously provided a desk and complimentary stationery for their clientele. Aunt Sophia regarded these amenities as her own, and spent two hours every week paying bills and writing letters. If, upon arrival, she had found *her* desk already occupied, she would simply have appealed to the usurper's sense of justice and reason.

In five minutes the desk would be vacated, and the distraught woman would be begging Aunt Sophia's forgiveness.

Before she could begin her labors, Aunt Sophia had to first do something with her mother. Since my grandmother was an avid people watcher, Aunt Sophia deposited her on the chintz settee across from the lounge door. "Are you all right, Ma? Ma! Are you all right?" Bubby looked up, nodded, and returned to her scrutiny of the ladies coming and going. She would remain in that spot transfixed, until Aunt Sophia finished her work, and came to retrieve her.

For many years after I left Baltimore, I received letters from Aunt Sophia that had been written on Hutzler's stationery. I always pictured her sitting at that desk as she wrote. During the incredible upheaval of the sixties, it was comforting to realize that *some* things never changed. That's why I was so surprised, the day they chose to make an exception.

I had been back from my honeymoon only a week or so, when Aunt Sophia called.

"Hi shmuggle-puggle. Would it be all right if Bubby and I stop by for a visit?"

I was dumbstruck! It was Thursday, and I wasn't even on their schedule! I may have turned twenty that summer, but to them I was the precocious two year old they still quoted with such pleasure.

"Remember honey, how you used to say, 'It's cold and *vindy* outside today'?"

Now that I was on my own, they needed to satisfy themselves that I was really "oh right," according to Bubby's vernacular. Stanley, my new husband was in graduate school, so we had rented a furnished efficiency near Johns Hopkins University. The building was called *The Bradford* and had been built in the 1920's as a hotel. It was famous for having housed two people whose behavior was sometimes notorious: Bugsy Siegel and F. Scott Fitzgerald.

Bubby at the Bradford

It was late afternoon when Bubby and Aunt Sophia appeared at my door. Bubby looked stricken, the way she did in the presence of wealth or great beauty. Apparently the tall Gothic exterior, and the carpeting in the lobby had impressed her. There was even an elevator that worked! Behind the square lenses of her old-fashioned wire-rimmed spectacles, Bubby's soft brown eyes looked so big, they threatened to obscure the rest of her.

She knew that buildings like this housed professional offices, but she hadn't known they housed dwellings. For ordinary people yet! She was overcome with the grandeur of it all.

Wordlessly, she handed me a square cardboard bakery box. Aunt Sophia automatically interpreted. "Bubby says, you and Stanley should live and be well till a hundred and twenty years," she took a breath, "and your life should be as sweet as these cookies!" Bubby smiled shyly. Her silences were always eloquent.

My friend Barbara happened to be visiting that same day. We had been sitting at the table talking when Aunt Sophia and Bubby arrived. Eager to practice my new role as hostess, I opened the box and offered the cookies to Barbara. They were my favorites, the kind we called chocolate splats.

"Help yourself," I suggested in my best lady-of-the-house-manner, hoping the cookies would keep her company while I led my doting relatives on the tour.

We began in the large living room, which doubled as the bedroom when the Murphy bed came down at night. The furnishings the management had provided were all clean and in good condition, but the style was reminiscent of the hotel's hey-day. Antiquated would be the *mot juste*.

Bubby wandered around reverently, touching the flowered upholstery, patting the flowered draperies, admiring the flowered rug. She exclaimed over the high ceilings, and applauded the cross ventilation. From the corner of my eye I watched her run her finger along the window sill—checking for *schmutz*.

Obediently she padded after me into our adequate no-frills bathroom. I prayed that the giant cockroach who divided his time between our apartment and our next door neighbor's, would not choose this particular moment to make his appearance. Bubby would have been horrified! In her mind, cockroaches were synonymous with dirt.

We approached the tiny kitchen and eating area. Bubby's face shone with wonder, as if she were viewing the Palace of the Czar. Her expression said, *Everything I went through was worth it. My granddaughter has it all.*

Aunt Sophia, who always had her own agenda, had deserted us somewhere between the living room and the bathroom. Now she stood in the kitchen doorway, feet planted firmly behind Barbara's chair, under the apparent delusion that she was invisible! Her expression was ferocious. She mouthed words at me in an exaggerated manner, and gesticulated violently with her hands. *Was she having some kind of a fit?*

My friend, unaware of the drama unfolding behind her, continued placidly eating. Aunt Sophia jabbed her finger toward Barbara, then the cookies, then jerked her thumb over her shoulder toward the kitchen. Aha! Now I understood. In her usual subtle way, Aunt Sophia was indicating that in her opinion, Barbara was eating too many of *my* cookies. I was to remove them before they disappeared altogether.

With enormous effort I managed to keep a blank face. Had I acknowledged Aunt Sophia's gyrations, Barbara would have looked behind her to see what was happening. Instead I turned, and quickly left the room.

Aunt Sophia was not discouraged. She believed that a campaign once embarked upon must never be abandoned. Undaunted, she changed tack.

Suddenly materializing in front of Barbara, she began. "Soooo, honey. Do you live far from here?"

Without giving Barbara time to answer, Aunt Sophia charged in for the kill.

"It's getting *late*, don't you think? You don't want to drive home in the *dark*, do you?"

Barbara got the hint. Reluctantly she said her goodbyes, and left. Aunt Sophia peered mournfully into the now empty cookie box. "Look at *that*," she lamented. "We bring you cookies, *and she eats them all!* You should have taken them away honey. You should have taken them away."

That was the closest Aunt Sophia ever came to criticizing me.

Bubby and the Brisket

Bubby's unhappiness with her appearance was about more than just being "fat." She was also of two minds about her nose. When it allowed her to enjoy wonderful fragrances, she regarded it as a blessing, but whenever she looked in a mirror, she declared it a curse!

Her nose was short and a little bit wide, but she saw it as big and ugly. Worse! It was the ugliest nose she had ever seen! God forbid, she should live to see her nose reproduced on the face of an innocent baby. As each new infant came into the family, Bubby would hasten to ask two questions. First, "Is the baby healthy?" Then, "Does she have my nose?"

Assurances from the family were meaningless. Bubby had to inspect each nose for herself.

We'd hold our collective breath as Bubby approached each crib, her face solemn, her forehead furrowed. If the nose passed muster, she smiled beatifically. If not, her eyes filled with tears. "Poor ting, poor ting, she be like me," she'd intone, in a voice from the tomb. And nothing we said would console her.

The afternoon Bubby came to the Bradford, her nose was in its blessing mode.

"Vat you cooking, Jo-vennala?" she asked inhaling with pleasure.

"Brisket, Bubby."

She inhaled more deeply. "Vondaful, Jo-vennala, it gone be delicious!"

She padded after me into my tiny kitchen and hovered over the open oven door. As I lifted the top of the roasting pan, a pungent aroma wafted up filling our nostrils. The roast was an enticing shade of brown. Morsels of onion, carrot and potato poked out of the rich bubbling sauce. I basted the meat.

"Beautiful!" she exclaimed, gazing raptly at the brisket. I might have been basting the Mona Lisa. Then came the question I was dreading.

"Is kosher, Jo-vennala?"

I paused. Then, reluctantly, "No Bubby, I got it at the A&P." I waited for the lightning to flash and the thunder to roar.

"How much you pay?" she asked, taking me by surprise.

When I told her she replied, "You be smart. *Di choleria* (the butcher) charge too much and da meat be tough like *anating*." She made a sour face.

"But Bubby, *You* can buy meat from the A&P too!"

"No," she said, sad with resignation. "God vould punish me." She was convinced that this was true.

I never was able to understand why it was all right for me to buy and consume non-kosher meat, when it wasn't all right for her. Why wouldn't God punish me?

Bubby seemed to believe that for someone else, He might make allowances, but not for her. She therefore chose to live as if the Celestial Countenance was focussed permanently on her.

At the end of the visit, in the midst of our goodbyes, Bubby took my hand in her humble way and kissed it. She looked earnestly up into my eyes. Her voice quavered with emotion. "It be beautiful, Jo-vennala. It be beautiful!" I think she was talking about more than just the apartment or the brisket. I think she was talking about my life.

Her heartfelt proclamation reminded me of a favorite passage in Genesis: "And God looked at what He had made and called it good."

Bubby the Believer

For an Orthodox Jew, my grandmother was very catholic in her belief system. Recklessly, she combined orthodox law with magic and superstition in a desperate effort to exert some semblance of control over her life. Next to survival, her main interest was safeguarding her loved ones, and she would stop at nothing to achieve that goal.

Bubby didn't view her use of superstition as being disloyal to the tenets of Judaism. Rather, she regarded it as extra insurance. After all, "It couldn't hurt."

Because she saw God as vengeful and quixotic, she continued to practice Orthodox laws and customs. Had she stoppped, she knew Retribution would be Swift and Terrible. She feared God, but *He* was too mysterious and remote to protect her.

Instead she protected herself—by manipulating the Evil Eye. With the Evil Eye, Bubby was very familiar. It was always there—right over her shoulder—watching, listening, ready to pounce! She had to be alert at all times. Avoiding the wrath of God, and outwitting the Evil Eye, kept Bubby hopping. She'd never heard of Satchel Paige, but she followed his philosophy: "Keep moving, and never look back 'cause something might be gaining on you."

According to Bubby, the Evil Eye had followed her all the way from Russia. Fortunately, along with her Sabbath candlesticks, she had also packed her charms and incantations. Her candlesticks enjoyed a place of honor on the sideboard, and were lovingly polished before each Sabbath. Her charms and incantations, although not visible to the naked eye, were also on-hand, accessible at a moment's notice. They were used so often they *never* needed polishing.

Bubby and Aunt Sophia believed that words contained magical powers which could be used for good or evil. One wrong word could bring disaster. If I said, "That baby girl has the face of an angel," Bubby would become frantic.

"Pooh, pooh, pooh, take it back, honey, take it back," Aunt Sophia would plead. God Forbid, the Evil Eye might hear and turn the little one into a *real* angel.

They were also convinced that if a child said something, it came true. Their definition of "child" encompassed anyone in the succeeding generations. Therefore at the age of thirty, to them I was still a child.

Whenever Bubby got sick Aunt Sophia would say, "I wish she'll be well." If I didn't immediately echo that wish, she would urge, "Say it, honey."

I would repeat, "I wish she'll be well."

"Say 'Bubby' honey, say the *name*," she would implore.

"I wish *Bubby* will be well."

"Say it again. Say it louder. Say the whole thing!"

"I WISH BUBBY WILL BE WELL!"

Three times was the magic number. Only then would she be satisfied. Aunt Sophia repeated some form of this litany often throughout her lifetime. Sometimes she'd say, "I wish it'll be nothing," or "I wish it doesn't happen," or even,"I wish it isn't true." After each fervent declaration she'd remind me,*"Say it!"*

So why did I wonder at the mysterious happenings of that muggy July afternoon? Baltimore, in the throes of summer—when the air is so thick with moisture, even the bees are too breathless to buzz. I was recovering from the Caesarian birth of my first daughter, relaxing with my mother on her patio. Limp as cooked spaghetti, we lay plastered to our chairs. Only my newborn's fretful rustlings disturbed the unnatural quiet, as Missy snuffled and snorted in her bassinet.

Suddenly, a clarion voice shattered our reverie. "We just stopped by for a visit! Mommy wants to see the new baby. Is it all right?"

Mother blanched.

There stood Bubby on the sidewalk, mutely clutching her black leather pocketbook. Behind her loomed Aunt Sophia. Still talking. "You don't mind, do you Mary?" Without waiting for an answer, she continued. "Boy, it's some hot today! Isn't this some scorcher?"

Peeling herself out of her chair, my mother went to kiss her mother. "Hello, Ma. *Vus machts-du?*"

Meanwhile, Aunt Sophia bustled over to me, Uncle Irvin loping behind her. "How do you feel honey, are you all right?" She stooped to kiss me.

Bubby darted over, pecked me on the cheek, then made a bee-line for the baby. Gazing through the mosquito netting, she stood transfixed—her face suffused by a luminous glow. "*Oy, ken ahora, a shayna punnim,*" she crooned to my restless new treasure. "*A mazel auf dir.*" "*A mazel auf dine keppala!*"

My grandmother turned toward me, her eyes sparkling with pleasure. "She be beautiful, Jo-Vennala. She be beautiful. *Ken ahora!*"

Neither Bubby nor Aunt Sophia ever gave a compliment without adding *ken ahora*. They were afraid the Evil Eye might hear, and punish the one who'd been complimented. When Missy was little, we had to use these magic words so often, Uncle Irvin changed her middle name from Susan to *Ken Ahora!*

After Bubby had drunk her fill of this wondrous child, she trotted over to a chair and perched on the edge. Bubby always perched. She was afraid to take up too much room.

Aunt Sophia, jangling and bangling, stowed her own and Bubby's voluminous pocketbooks, and subsided into an arm chair. Uncle Irvin, after stopping to kiss my mother, and peek at the baby, swooped down to kiss me. Having completed the preliminaries, he stretched out in the plastic lounge chair and went to sleep.

The afternoon wore on, heavy with humidity. Mother stared into space. Bubby mused, smiling and nodding. Uncle Irvin dozed.

Minutes dragged by, sodden and lethargic. We sat steeping in our own sweat; soggy as forgotten teabags left to languish in the pot. Silence thickened around us.

A fly landed on Uncle Irvin. Aunt Sophia swiped at it, her bracelets jingling. Behind her netting, Missy began to *kvetch*.

More flies appeared. Aunt Sophia unfolded a cocktail napkin, and covered what she could of her husband's expansive face. A fly buzzed by Uncle Irvin's temple. Aunt Sophia pushed the napkin higher. Another went for the cleft in his chubby chin. She slid the paper back, grazing his cheek with her long enameled nail. Uncle Irvin grimaced. The napkin shifted.

Pulling first one end and then another, Aunt Sophia finally solved the problem by tucking one of the corners into the nearest of Uncle Irvin's ears.

His querulous voice floated up through the paper. "What 're you *doin'*, Soph?"

With great reluctance she removed the offending napkin, exposing her husband's flushed and dripping face. "Look at that," she exclaimed. "Irvin woke up already!" Her voice was filled with honest wonder.

While Aunt Sophia continued to puzzle over this amazing coincidence, Mother excused herself, returning with a large pitcher of icy lemonade. A neighbor, Mrs. F. stopped by. "Can I see the baby?"

"Sure," I agreed.

Bubby the Believer

Missy began to fuss just as Mrs. F. approached the bassinet. When the poor woman got close enough to peer through the netting, Missy's fussing escalated into shrieks. Bubby snapped to attention. Grasping the situation in a flash, she hopped off her perch, and hit the ground running.

Before the surprised neighbor could close her mouth, Bubby had scooped up the baby, trotted up the back steps, and disappeared into the kitchen. BANG! went the screen door. Taking a little less time than it took the Children of Israel to find their way out of the desert, Aunt Sophia gathered herself together, rose majestically, and followed Bubby.

I looked at my mother. She rolled her eyes heavenward and shrugged. My curiosity got the best of me. Struggling out of my chair, I limped up the stairs after Aunt Sophia.

When I got to the kitchen, Bubby was standing by the sink, cradling my now hysterical child in her soft, protective arms. Missy's crumpled face was scarlet, her tiny hands fisted with fury. Bubby was leaning over her crooning unintelligible syllables, then licking Missy's forehead.

I stared at my grandmother, dumbfounded! Aunt Sophia watched from a few feet away. When she saw the expression on my face, her legs buckled and she rocked with silent laughter. "Don't be mad, honey, don't be mad," she gasped. Her eyes streamed with tears.

"What's going on?" I demanded.

Aunt Sophia tried to control her euphoria. "Bubby says the neighbor looked at Missy with strange eyes," she burbled, "and put an *ahora* (an evil curse) on her. Bubby is breaking the spell. She's spitting out the Devil."

I wasn't angry, I was amazed. Here it was 1960 and my grandmother was performing magic in my mother's kitchen on *my* baby daughter! I watched Bubby's face. She actually *believed* in this mumbo-jumbo!

Finishing the incantation, my grandmother turned beseeching eyes on me. "Jo-Vennala," she admonished. "Don't let strange eyes look auf her *anymore!*"

"I won't, Bubby," I stammered.

Solemnly, she handed me my now calm and peaceful infant. She straightened her slip and patted her hair. Then, trailed by Aunt Sophia, she marched quietly back to her perch, to await the next emergency.

War, disease, death, even bad weather, Bubby and Aunt Sophia took responsibility for them all. Ceaselessly they fought against the ravages of Evil, endeavoring to impose order on a chaotic world. As far as I could determine, the world continued unaffected, but Bubby and Aunt Sophia evidently took their readings from a different barometer.

Bubby Goes to Bay Shore

Certain things in nature are fixed and unchanging, like the regularity of the tides, and the rhythm of the seasons. We find comfort in their predictability. Certain things in my family were also fixed and unchanging, like Bubby and Aunt Sophia. Their predictability was not always so comforting.

They responded to the overwhelmingness of life by ritualizing it. *Everything* was ritualized. Once a procedure was adopted, it could be deviated from only under *dire* circumstances. Deviations required rituals of their own. Thus the simplest things became extremely complicated. A trip to the beach, for example, was a *gantseh megilla!*

In my family, summer was not official until the arrival of the summer solstice. Since swimming was a summertime activity, going to the beach was not permitted before the twenty-first of June, even if the mercury soared to a hundred. Sticky and irritable children who begged to be taken to the beach before they "melted," were told by equally sticky and irritable adults, "It's not summer yet!"

When the eagerly awaited solstice finally arrived, Bubby was right behind it. She'd appear at our door on a hot Sunday morning, flushed and panting, after covering the block and a half between her house and ours at a very brisk trot. Reaching into the pocket of her pink flowered housedress, she'd extract the first clean handkerchief of the day. "It be hot!" she'd exclaim, dabbing vigorously at her dripping forehead. Then she'd smile apologetically, as if somehow it was her fault.

"Marala?" she'd address my mother in her tentative quavery voice, "a myby ve go today by dem beach?" Bubby's usually solemn brown eyes shone with anticipation.

"Yeah, let's go!"

"Oh boy, the beach!"

"Let's go, let's go, let's go!" whooped my brother Larry and I. *Help us coax,* I signaled Gischa, our older sister, but she pretended not to notice, and pursed her lips. *How juvenile,* she must be thinking. Lately, *juvenile* had become her favorite word.

We turned to Daddy, "Please, please, please?" we begged.

Daddy's eyes grew dreamy. He licked his lips as if he could already taste the salt water, then filled his lungs with imaginery sea air. "Sure, let's go," he agreed, then ducked his head and added, "If it's all right with Mother."

Five pairs of eyes swiveled toward Mother. *Say yes, say yes, say yes!* But Mother didn't notice. She was staring at something deep inside that made her eyes bulge, her hands clench, and her delicate mouth clamp shut. The anticipation of spending a whole day with her family usually had this effect on her.

She knew what she'd be letting herself in for. Getting our family to the beach was like relocating a military complex. Bay Shore was an hour's drive away. If we were to get there before late afternoon, Mother would have to single-handedly synchronize, organize, and mobilize two households; Bubby's, and our own. Still, if she said no, she would never hear the end of it.

Emerging from her coma, she looked at our expectant faces. "God give me strength!" she breathed. She squared her shoulders, and—like our patriarch Moses—resigned herself to a reluctant command.

Mother dispatched Bubby to alert the troops. "Ma, tell Sophia to be ready in one hour. Irvin can drive you all back here, and you'll follow us to the shore." She knew it was faster to send Bubby than to use the telephone.

Excited by the prospect of an outing, my grandmother streaked back to Oakley Avenue, her short legs pumping. She had been up since dawn and had already cleaned the whole house. She would find my grandfather sipping ginger ale in the sun parlour, his thick pajama-clad body wedged in his favorite wicker chair. He would be reading the *Yiddishe Forverts,* and listening to his floor-model Philco. First came the snappy Klezmer music, then a robust immigrant voice would boom, *"Dis is Net Yungelson und di Yiddishe Radio Stunde!"*

Zady always responded with one of his mammoth stentorian belches, "Ooh *wah* hoo!" He, like everyone else in our family, was a martyr to gas.

"*Mic-hel*?" Bubby would interrupt. "*Mir gaen by dem beach, mach shnell*!" Without waiting for Zady to answer, she'd charge upstairs to find her son-in-law.

"Urbin?" Bubby tapped timidly at the bathroom door, behind which Uncle Irvin was peacefully reading. "*Mir gaen by dem beach, mach shnell*!"

Two down, only one to go!

Bubby didn't have to run to find her daughter. All she had to do was wait, Aunt Sophia would eventually drift by. She was as regular as the number five streetcar. Had Bubby been able to tell time, she could have set her watch by her.

Although by now it was nearly noon, Aunt Sophia still roamed the halls like Lucia, her pink nightgown billowing behind her. Her pale face, studded with last night's wrinkle plasters, was a study in vague concentration. Back and forth she wandered, struggling to bridge the chasm between asleep and awake. Her voluptuous golden tresses lay flattened against her skull, captured under an ugly brown hairnet. Pointed metal clips poked and glinted through the netting like stars in a midnight sky. Morning did not become Aunt Sophia.

"Sophn!" Bubby called, breaking through the sound barrier, "*Mir gaen by dem beach! Mach shnell*!!" She may as well have talked to her rose bushes.

Zady remained in the sun parlor listening and belching. Uncle Irvin vacated the "reading room," but continued reading. Aunt Sophia gathered a few "necessities," ambled into the bathroom, and locked the door. Bubby grabbed some towels, then headed for the cedar chest to round up their suits.

Meanwhile, back at our house my mother, whom Aunt Sophia called The General, was issuing orders.

"Kit!" (to my father) "Go clean out the car."

"Jo-Ann and Larry, get the bathing bag, suits and towels."

"Gischa. I need help in the kitchen."

My father, delighted not to have drawn k.p., attacked the car with gusto. The insurance company he worked for generated enormous amounts of paper. Daddy saved every scrap and stored them all in cartons on the back seat. This was the perfect time, he decided, not only to clear space for us, but to clean out the cartons. Before he could decide what to keep, and what to throw away, he first had to read *every paper*. Daddy would finish cleaning out our car about the same time Aunt Sophia would emerge from her bathroom.

But Larry and I never learned. Frantic to get to the beach as soon as possible, we flew up the stairs. Tearing through the rooms, we grabbed towels, and our own suits, and stuffed them into the battered brown bathing bag.

Schlepping our load between us, we charged into Mother's room. Heaving with all our might, we pried up the top of the massive cedar chest. Peee Ewww! Our noses burned from that pungent aroma. Larry supported the lid, while I whipped through the scratchy layers of woolens, my eyes watering from the acrid fumes.

Mother's navy blue suit with the white rope trim, and Daddy's short black trunks with the metal belt were way at the bottom. I yanked them out, just as the lid slipped through Larry's sweaty fingers and slammed shut. Jamming the woolen suits in on top of ours, we raced down the steps and out to the car, bumping our bulging burden behind us.

"We're ready" we chorused, dropping the bag on the sidewalk. Daddy, absorbed in his papers, didn't respond. Throwing the front seat forward, we shoved the cartons aside, and clambered in. It was like climbing into a furnace.

Time passed. A merciless sun bombarded the black exterior of our aged '35 Plymouth. Sweat peppered our shiny faces and dribbled from the corners of our eyes.

Daddy read on. We sat there listening to the rattle of his papers. Perspiration skittered down our itchy bodies, and spread into little puddles behind our sticky knees. Soggy as water-logged wash rags, we had begun to leak. "When are we gonna *go*, already?"

Larry added his two cents to mine. "I'm hot," he complained.

Daddy said nothing.

"I thought we were going to the beach!"

But Daddy continued reading. Couldn't *he* feel the heat? Couldn't *he* hear the nagging?

After what seemed like a week, he came to.

"Go see if Mother needs any help," he instructed. I peeled myself off the upholstery, and shot out of the car.

Galloping up the stone steps, I flung open the screen door, and zoomed into the house like Roadrunner. Ugh! The heat hit me like a blow. It must have been a hundred and five in there! Mother was in our tunnel of a kitchen, imprisoned in the tiny space that passed for a corridor between the table and the sink. Surrounding her were half the contents of the pantry and refrigerator. Before her loomed the family picnic basket, its giant maw yawning wide. Behind her crouched the empty gallon jug. Flanking the jug like forlorn sentries, were two melting trays of ice. Their frosty tears oozed into an ever-widening pool.

Mother looked like a volcano with indigestion. I could practically see the #@!?!!! marks ballooning above her frazzled head. *Everyone* had deserted her, including my sister. Gischa, like Aunt Sophia, had retreated to her sanctuary, the bathroom. Once she disappeared behind that door, no communication from this planet could reach her!

I watched Mother nervously, feeling a warning quiver on my internal Mom-o-Meter. I knew she hated the heat. I knew she hated that claustrophobic kitchen. But more than the heat and the kitchen combined, she hated family trips to the beach. Especially if she had to organize them!

Mother wasn't packing lunch, she was outfitting an entire regiment! Not only was she providing plenty of wholesome, nutritious food for nine people, she was keeping track of each one's personal taste. And from all seven of the Basic Food Groups! She was following the amounts prescribed by Adele Davis, *and* the U. S. Government's Required Daily Allowances. No wonder she was frustrated!

In addition, she was trying to think of every piece of equipment the nine of us might possibly require, in this world or the next. Like chairs and blankets for us to sit on, hats, jackets, and lotion to protect our skin, bathing caps to protect our ears, sunglasses to protect our eyes, and beach shoes to protect our feet. And don't forget the inner tube! Even the grown-ups vied for turns with that!

Bubby had taught her daughter well. We would be prepared for anything, including acts of God, and unexpected cataclysms of nature. The Evil Eye was watching. We must leave nothing to chance. General

Eisenhower's troops prepared less for the invasion of Normandy than we did for a day at the seashore.

The heavy moisture-laden air pressed down upon us like a giant thumb. Mother's fists clenched and began to shake. Her mouth began to work. I took one look and hot-footed it back to my father.

"You'd better get in there fast," I told him. "Mother is about to blow!"

My words, and the emotion propelling them, roused my father the way an air raid siren rouses a sleeping warden. He started, then bit his lip. The tight skin on his forehead crumpled into furrows as he disengaged himself from his papers, and backed quickly out of the car. Head down, shoulders hunched forward, he bolted toward the house—a condemned man hurrying to meet his executioner.

I climbed back in beside Larry. Suffocating in the car beat getting zapped in one of Mother's explosions. When she went off, even the fallout could kill!

Mother's fury burst through the open windows like machinegun fire. Her voice throbbed with the intensity of a detonated bomb. Larry and I huddled closer, gluing ourselves together with our sweat. Higher and higher soared Mother, spiraling into the stratosphere, a defective rocket run amok. *Please...just let us get there,* I prayed.

For one minute there was perfect quiet. Then...Slam! went the windows. Bang! went the front door. Mother stomped down the steps, arms swinging, swooping the heavy basket from side to side. Her jaw had forged into iron, but her eyes shone with a peculiar light. She was Ingrid Bergman, marching bravely toward the stake.

"Make sure the door is locked," Mother snapped over her shoulder at my father. The hair on the back of my neck stood up. She plunked down the basket, and reached for the door handle. I shivered. *Some ride this is going to be!* Mentally, I rolled my eyes.

Daddy, looking as if he had just stepped on a land mine, tap danced after Mother. Knees buckling, legs pumping, he lunged down the pavement toward us, clutching the massive ice chest to his heart. The skin on his bony arms stretched tight across his biceps, making his muscles ripple and his veins pop up.

Tripping daintily after Daddy was Gischa, alias Scarlet O'Hara. She swept down the walk as if both sides were lined with adoring beaus. My sister, resplendent in green ruffles, smiled her mysterious smile, and inclined her head, acknowledging the clamour of the multitudes. In one hand she carried the gallon jug, but away from her body—as if its battered condition might somehow infect her. In the other she carried her beach things, which Larry and I were never allowed to touch. We might give her cooties, or something!

Gischa handed the jug to Daddy, who was trying to cram a hundred cubic feet of equipment into a fifty cubic foot space. Climbing gracefully into the back seat, she elbowed me aside, as if I were a carton of Daddy's papers, and plunked herself firmly next to the window. *Gischa,* who couldn't stand for a single hair on her head to blow! I, on the other hand, would have welcomed a tornado. Now I'd have to share with my brother. *Would she trade for Boardwalk and Park Place?*

Scarlet arranged her ruffles, patted her dark curls sweetly and fixed me with a menacing eye. "Keep your dirty shoes off me," she snarled, drawing an invisable line between us. One more glance in the rear view mirror, and she composed herself to wait. Sheesh, what a pain!

Daddy shoved in the last of the luggage, and wrestled the trunk shut. Wham! Everybody jumped. It was like a bomb going off behind us. He climbed behind the wheel with his eyes down, and his lower lip jutting. Mother sat beside him, back rigid, eyes forward, tightening the tension screw another notch.

Bubby goes to Bay Shore

Larry and I peered at Bubby's house through the dusty back window. I balanced on my bony knees; he stood on the seat beside me. Suddenly there it was! Zady's old Dodge, shimmering up the incandescent street like a ghostly galleon. "They're coming, they're coming," we shouted. Larry hopped up and down with excitement. My feet flailed in every direction. "Jo-Ann!" thundered my distraught sister, yanking her skirt clear of my offending shoes.

Uncle Irvin nosed the green car in behind us. His arm, resting on the open window, looked caramel against his crisp white shirt. The ever present cigarette dangled comfortably between his thick short fingers. He might have been at home, relaxing in his easy chair. One blue eye winked as soon as he saw me. Uncle Irvin's version of a salute.

Next to Uncle Irvin sat Aunt Sophia, her golden hair gleaming in the sun. Regal, and serene as Cleopatra, she waited for him to barge her up the Nile.

Zady had sprawled his bulk across the back seat, like an aging lion. Bubby perched beside him like a little mouse. Wisps of hair lay plastered to her flushed forehead, and hung in limp brown strands from her soggy bun. Daddy yelled last minute instructions to Uncle Irvin. Thumbs up came the mimed reply. I heard the key turn in our ignition. The motor roared to life, and we were off!

I expected to be cooler once we started moving, but the sun, now directly overhead, made the air inside the car thick with heat. We crawled along at thirty-five miles per hour, sweat pouring off us in bucketfuls. It was like travelling in a Turkish bath.

"Open the window, I'm dying!"
"Close the window, my hair!"
"Are we there yet, ? I'm thirsty."
"The lemonade's in the trunk. You'll have to wait."
"Are we almost there?"
"Almost," fibbed my father.

Before long we were one of the long line of bumper-to-bumper cars inching ponderously through the glare. Sometimes the traffic eased, and Uncle Irvin pulled alongside us. Larry and I waved like crazy. Aunt Sophia smiled and waved back. Sometimes she blew kisses. Not a hair of Uncle Irvin's *Vitalisized* pomadour had wilted. He looked as cool as if he had just gone for a refreshing swim.

Daddy, who had perfect pitch, but could never remember lyrics, started singing. "If you wore a la-la, and I wore a la-la, and la-la-la-la-la-la." After a few minutes, Mother joined in, singing off key, but enunciating every word.

"That ain't the way it goes, Mary. Sing it like this: la-la-la," he corrected.

Mother subsided. Daddy, unaware that he had hurt her feelings, warbled on. Gischa picked up the harmony, and together they finished *If You Wore A Tulip* and segued into *Wait Till The Sun Shines Nellie*.

Larry, who didn't enjoy singing, was bored. "I don't have anything to do," he whined.

"We're almost there," came the automatic response.

"I'm hungry," he persisted.

"The food is in the trunk. We'll have a nice picnic when we get there."

I decided to add my voice to the festivities. "I don't feel so good."

"Lean out the window and get some air."

"It's *my* turn to sit by the window."

"No it isn't. You just had a turn. It's *mine*."

"Get your feet off me."

"Then open the window. I'm broiling!"

"No! No! My hair!"

"I have to go pish."

Daddy waggled his hand out the window, signalling frantically. Wrenching the car to the side of the road, he stopped. Uncle Irvin glided in behind us. Mother and Larry disappeared behind a tree while everyone else got out to stretch. Zady, who liked to watch us from a distance, limped over to the shade, propping himself against a tree. His hooded eyes glittered like a cat's. Zady always looked as if he were telling himself a joke, and we were the punch line.

Aunt Sophia fanned her generous bosom, making her bracelets clank.

"Whew, it's some hot! Isn't it, honey?"

I nodded, rolling my eyes.

Bubby smiled. "It be hot," she agreed mopping her face with yet another sodden handkerchief. But behind the magnified lens of her wire-rimmed glasses, her eyes danced.

Daddy dug through the trunk, excavating the jug, and we gulped down the icy nectar.

"Some traffic, huh Kit?" Uncle Irvin looked fresh and unruffled as ever.

"God sakes! I never saw anything like it!"

Feeling cooler, and a little more energetic, we piled back in our cars for the last leg of our trip. We bobbed along in a sea of dusty cars. Very little air moved, and what did move was hot. *Weren't we ever going to get there?*

All of a sudden, Daddy inhaled sharply. "I smell the ocean," he proclaimed, his voice rising with excitement.

Mother, Daddy, Larry, and I poked our heads out the windows, pulling in deep drafts of fresh air. The salt made my nose tingle.

"Yeah, yeah, I smell it. The ocean."

"Yayy, the ocean, the ocean. We're almost there!"

We inhaled deeply, filling our lungs with the magic elixir.

There was a quickening in the car. Anticipation was up, all discomforts were forgotten.

Even Gischa put her nose out the window. She sniffed delicately, using both hands to hold on to her hair.

"Did we bring salt and pepper?" Now that we were getting close, Mother was beginning to organize her mind.

"Did anyone remember towels? What about a bottle opener? Why am I the only one who worries about these things?"

"There's the bridge," Daddy announced, pointing triumphantly.

Everyone followed Daddy's finger. We were almost there! My excitement mounted with each bump of our tires as we lumbered foreward over the narrow wooden planks. Scooting to the edge of my seat, I assumed the sprinter's position. I would be ready the second we landed, to hit that beach.

"Kit, what's that smoke coming out of the hood?"

Daddy took his eyes off the stream of traffic and followed Mother's pointing finger.

"God sakes, Mary! That ain't smoke; it's steam! The radiator's overheating!"

He yanked the car onto the shoulder of the bridge, accompanied by a loud chorus of "ooohhh nooo's" contributed by my brother and me. Daddy leaped into the oncoming traffic, ignoring Mother's, "Kit! Watch out for the cars!" Mother, Larry, and I craned to watch. Daddy raced to the front of the car, jerked open the latch and flung up the hood. A geyser of white steam shot heavenward. Snatching the support stick out of its holder, he jammed it against the hood.

He stood back a moment, hands on hips, watching the spewing plume. Then dancing with impatience, he began to pace. His splutterings ran a close second to the overheated radiator. "Durn thing! God sakes! Can you imagine that?"

Once again, Uncle Irvin pulled in behind us. Steam was shooting out of his radiator too. Swinging his two hundred and fifty pound body out of the Dodge with the grace of a dancer, he strolled forward, and raised its hood. Then he sauntered toward my father, smiling and winking at me as he passed. Uncle Irvin did not regard an overheated radiator on a hot day as a punishment from God. He knew the situation was temporary, and was prepared to wait till the cars cooled down. Uncle Irvin was a very patient man. He had to be, or he could never have lived with Aunt Sophia.

Uncle Irvin patted my father on the shoulder. "Calm down, Kit." But Daddy was so taut he could have launched arrows. His Indian brown body was arched forward like a bow. His fists flailed at his sides, and the veins in his arms bulged like rope. Uncle Irvin pointed to the ever increasing number of cars moving to the side of the bridge. They resembled a line of beached whales, each one spouting steam. Ours was not the only family chosen for this indignity. As soon as he saw the others, Daddy's fists uncurled and his shoulders relaxed.

The men waited in the sun, while the rest of us stayed in the cars, stewing in our own juices. The lulling murmur of Uncle Irvin's voice was punctuated by an occasional "God sakes!" from my father, but it no longer carried its original sizzle.

Inside the car, Larry and I reprised the Anvil chorus.

"What's taking so long?"

"When are we *going* already?"

Absorbed in her own misery, my mother could no longer hear us, and Gischa, as usual, had disappeared at will. I turned up the volume a smidgeon. It was bad enough being uncomfortable, I wasn't about to suffer alone.

"It's too hot, I can't stand it!

Silence.

"I'm itching all over. I'm sticking to the seat!"

No response.

"If I don't get out of here soon, I'll throw up!"

Gischa returned to Earth briefly to hiss. "God, are you a *kvetch!*"

Mother took up the refrain. "If that kvetching doesn't stop this *minute*," she began, in that threatening alto tone of hers, "I'm going to..." Her voice wobbled up an octave and crashed on the last two words, "... **commit murder!**"

She hadn't actually mentioned me by name, but I was pretty certain whom she had in mind.

Fortunately, the radiators cooled down just as Mother's temper heated up. It had taken twenty minutes, but it seemed like a year.

We rolled over the last of the bridge, and on through the gateway to Bay Shore Park. Hurray! Victory is ours! Larry and I burst into a rousing chorus of "We're here, because we're here, because we're here, because we're here ..." Daddy pulled into a parking space. Uncle Irvin slid in beside us.

The cars may have been parked, but my motor was still running. I wanted out *right now!* But it was not to be. This stupid car had only two doors! I'd have to wait for Mother to vacate. I considered diving through the open back window, but rejected it. I might decapitate myself, then Mother would really kill me. Instead, I waited for her to untangle her stiff muscles—one cramped vertebra at a time, while I kicked the back of her seat providing a rhythmic accompaniment.

As soon as she was out of the way, I shot the seat forward and leaped to the ground. Larry scrambled after me. Daddy jumped out and whizzed around to unlock the trunk. Gischa gathered herself together and stepped serenely into the sunshine, looking as if she had just been delivered by the dry cleaners.

Uncle Irvin slid, Bubby hopped, and Zady eased himself out of the Dodge, then waited, in the blistering sun, for Aunt Sophia. Waiting for Aunt Sophia was a full-time job, like waiting for the *mashiach*.

"Let's go, let's go," Larry and I yipped, our voices shrill with exasperation. We clutched our suits and towels, straining our bodies toward the bath-house which looked like it was at least a mile away. But the family, as usual, had a different agenda. First we had to unpack the cars and take *everything* to the picnic area. Everyone but Zady had to schlepp.

Now a discussion ensued. Who should carry what? Everyone had an opinion. These discussions occurred often in my family. They tended to become both lengthy and passionate. To save time, we developed a system. Instead of everyone listening while one person spoke, we let everybody speak and nobody listened. Like the opera.

"Listen, Kit, I think we should ..."
"Naw, that ain't the way ..."
"Maybe if we ..."
"For God's sake, Soph ..."
"A myby ..."
"It's *hot* out here. Come *on* already!"

Finally, we divided up all the gear. Mother, Aunt Sophia, Larry and I piled hats on our heads, hung towels around our necks, and draped robes over our shoulders like disheveled Bedouins. Mother and Gischa each carried a folding chair and lugged the family bathing bag between them. Bubby grabbed the blankets, Larry carried his sand toys, and I wore the prized innertube around my middle, like a giant bagel. The hole was so wide, and I was so skinny, I was always in danger of slipping through. I needed both hands just to hold it up. Aunt Sophia juggled a bulky assortment of bags and bundles. Daddy and Uncle Irvin hefted the ice chest, the gallon jug, and the giant picnic basket that, by now, weighed more than I did.

We fanned out in random formation, our feet sucking the shifting sand. Hats tilted, robes dangling, towels flapping, onward we trudged. Zady leaned forward on his cane, his bald head hidden under his squashed straw beach hat. Bubby, intent on her destination, raced ahead. Aunt Sophia, weaving back and forth with her uneven burden, began to chuckle. Daddy and Uncle Irvin lurched behind us clanking and swearing. We were on the move!

Arriving at the picnic area, we dumped our stuff on the first available table. Everyone sighed with relief. Bubby made a *tsekvetcheta punim*.

Aunt Sophia: "What's the matter, Ma?"

Bubby: "A myby it's too hot?" She wrinkled her nose and pointed to the sun.

Aunt Sophia: "Mommy says this table isn't good."

We picked up our belongings and moved to another table.

Mother: "What about this one, Ma?"

Bubby shook her head. We reshouldered our gear, and slogged onward.

"Here's a good one," someone offered. We hesitated while Bubby considered. Again she shook her head. Again we marched.

Uncle Irvin: "Here Ma, this is the best table!"

Bubby looked. She nodded. Thank God! We piled everything on the table.

Aunt Sophia: "I don't think this is good, we're in a draft here."

"A draft?" yelped Daddy. "How could we be in a draft? We're outside!"

Aunt Sophia shrugged her shoulders. "I don't know, maybe it wouldn't be good for Mommy."

"God Sakes!" Daddy exploded, but he knew he was beaten. Muttering under his breath, he grabbed the ice chest and lugged it to another table. This one was half shaded from the sun.

Mother: "Look at the flies, Kit, we're too close to the garbage cans."

Daddy's patience fizzled. "Aw for God's sakes Mary, a few flies ain't gonna hurt nobody!" With great gusto the operatic chorus swung into Act II. Eventually we settled on a table. God alone knows how.

By now we were starving, but we agreed to delay lunch for a "refreshing dip in the ocean." The food would taste better when we were cooler. Leaving the picnic things to reserve our table, we collected our beach stuff, and moved toward the bathhouse.

Hoisting the innertube over one shoulder, I dashed ahead, ecstatic to be free! I waited in line for a basket, then charged into an empty cubby, and rolled off my sweaty clothes in one continuous sweep. Without losing momentum, I attempted to leap into my bathing suit reversing that same sweeping motion. But fate was against me. My skin was so damp, the latex stuck to my legs. The harder I pulled, the faster it stuck. The suit stretched, but it wouldn't *go* anywhere. I wiggled my hips from side to side trying to loosen its hold on me, but the suit, like my family, only moved when it was ready.

Finally! I threw my tangled clothing into the basket and returned it to the counter girl in exchange for my clothes check. Stretching the elastic band over my ankle, I memorized my number, convinced that if I lost it, I would forfeit my clothes forever.

I passed Bubby on my way out. She was almost ready. Gischa and Aunt Sophia were just coming in.

Outside, the men stood in a circle, talking. Daddy and Uncle Irvin joked about how long women take to get dressed. I inhaled, filling my lungs with the tang of sea air, the earthy pungence of wet sand, and the acrid aroma of moth balls.

Larry and I moved into the shadow of the building, and traced designs in the sand with our toes. The cool satiny grains caressed my sweaty skin, responding to the slightest pressure. If only the family would move so willingly!

Bubby emerged from the bathhouse followed by Mother, then Gischa, and finally Aunt Sophia. Now the mothball aroma was everywhere! Daddy led the way to the beach, striding barefoot across the burning sand. Larry and I started after him, but very quickly yelped for help.

"Ow, ow, my feet! It's too hot to walk!" We hopped up and down, trying to keep our tender tootsies out of contact with the scorching sand.

Without breaking his stride Daddy called back, "Aw, what's the matter with you babies? A little heat ain't gonna hurt you!" He was moving so fast his pain didn't have time to register.

Aunt Sophia called, "Irv, Irv, the children!"

Uncle Irvin to the rescue. He bounded over, whisked Larry up under one arm and me and my inner tube under the other and took off after Daddy like Tarzan.

Bubby nearly matched his stride. It took more than hot sand to stop her! Aunt Sophia, standing for protection on someone else's blanket, called "Look at Mommy. Look how she runs!" Aunt Sophia crossed her legs, and doubled over with laughter.

Daddy had just finished arranging the blankets when we caught up with him.

Time out for an operatic encore.

"You're too close to the water. It's better over here."

"You're too far from the bathroom. Move it over here."

"Over there is too crowded, move it over here!"

No matter where he put the blankets, somebody objected. Finally we ageed, more or less, on a "perfect spot" and distributed our paraphernalia. The chairs for Bubby and Zady were unfolded and placed facing the water. The time for swimming was at hand. Atlantic Ocean—here we come!

No, not quite. Fate wasn't finished playing with us. In a flash, the brilliant sky turned inky black. Drops the size of quarters began to fall. Before we could move, the drops became a deluge. Yikes! Grabbing our towels, we headed for the pavillion. We huddled together under the thatched roof, shivering as a sudden gust chilled our rain-soaked skin. Our towels were drenched, but we pulled them closer about us. All except Gischa, who was using hers to protect her hair.

Bubby, sitting quietly in the midst of us, began to rock with silent laughter. Tears rolled down her wrinkled cheeks as she gasped out colorful Yiddish phrases, describing the anticipation, aggravation, and frustration we had had to endure that day. Her eyes sparkled as she recreated every nuance, capturing each of our eccentricities in her gentle, loving way.

"Look at you," she quavered in Yiddish, "Yir zest oyse vi oysgevaikte ketz!" (You look like a pack of half-drowned cats.)

Mother and Aunt Sophia laughed till they cried. Aunt Sophia had to cross her legs again. "She's afraid she'll pish in her pants," Uncle Irvin explained.

Mercifully, the shower was soon over, and the sun reappeared bright and hot. We strolled back to the picnic table, and this time put away a large meal. We took our time returning to our blankets. The water was off limits anyway, so why rush?

At the end of thirty minutes, Bubby walked into the ocean, stopping when the water reached her knees. Bending over, she splashed water on her bosom. "Ahhhhhhh! *a mechia.*" she crooned. Feeling braver, she pulled the top of her suit away, and dipped handfulls of the cooling fluid into her cleavage. "Ahhhhh...*a mechia. A shaynam mechia!*" Her face shone with a transcendent light. All long the water's edge were other elderly Jewish ladies about the size and shape of my grandmother, also dipping water into their cleavages and telling each other what a *mechia* it was.

Meanwhile, back at the blanket, Aunt Sophia began to squirm. When Bubby came back from her dip she asked, "Sophn, *vus a da mer?*" Aunt Sophia complained that her suit itched. Bubby offered to exchange with her. Since it was too far to walk to the bath house, they decided to make the switch underwater.

They waded in up to their armpits, and crouched over. Bubby was out of her suit in a second. Aunt Sophia, however, was *zoftig* and tended to float. As she pulled down the top of her suit, her generous breasts bobbed up to the surface. Now it was Uncle Irvin's turn to go *meshuga*.

"Soph!" he hollered, gesticulating wildly, "Get down Soph! Get down!"

When Aunt Sophia saw his face redden, and his eyes bulge, she began to laugh. She tried to stay underwater, but the laughter brought her up. Each time she surfaced, Uncle Irvin got more excited. He yelled and waved, and she laughed and bobbed. Bubby was still crouching in the water, holding her discarded suit. By now, Aunt Sophia was helpless with laughter. Between convulsions she unsuccessfully attempted to rein in her run-away breasts.

This *mishegas* continued for some time, much to the amusement of the onlookers who had been alerted by Uncle Irvin's apoplectic gyrations. Eventually, the suits were exchanged, and life returned to what is regarded in this family as normal.

The rest of the day passed without incident. We ate, sunbathed, and swam. After consuming a large dinner we changed back into our street clothes, packed up our gear, and headed home.

The sun was already down as we crossed over the bridge. We felt cleansed, inside and out, ironed smooth by the sun and the sea. The ride home was relaxing and peaceful. We chatted a little, reviewing the highlights of the day. Everything seemed much funnier in retrospect. When Daddy started singing, everyone joined in, including Mother. This time he didn't holler when she went off key. The evening air was soft and balmy, heavy with the sweetness of honeysuckle. Gischa rolled down her window so we could saturate our lungs.

About half-way home, we stopped at Emerson's Farm for ice cream. Aunt Sophia said, "Remember, honey?

When you were two years old? We bought you ice cream, and you said 'warm it up!'" Everyone laughed, as if we were hearing this story for the first time.

Sandy, sunburned and sleepy, we pulled in front of our darkened house. Daddy trotted out his usual line. "Looks like nobody's home," he cracked. Then he added, "That's a joke, son." Larry and Mother and I countered, "Oh, yeah? Well it t'aint funny Magee!" and collapsed in a fit of giggles.

For the last time that day, Uncle Irvin slid the Dodge in behind us. As we exchanged good night hugs and kisses, a gentle voice quavered in the darkness.

"A myby ve go again, next veek?"

"If We Live and Nothing Happens..."

Sophia

It would be impossible to talk about Aunt Sophia without including Bubby. They were part of each other, like Siamese twins who shared a single heart. Each was convinced that separation, whether physical or emotional, meant *death*!

On the surface, they had little in common. Bubby was fast and efficient; Aunt Sophia was slow and tentative. Around other people, Bubby was quiet, and self-effacing; Aunt Sophia was boisterous and irrepressible. Yet underneath they shared the same value system, the same world-view. More than that, the history they shared formed a bond which was so primitive, and so intense, both recognized it as irreversible.

Each one's hunger could only be satisfied by the other. They were the only members of their own exclusive club. Bubby loved all her children, but she *needed* Sophia. Over time, their individual roles blurred and became so blended, it was impossible to tell mother from daughter.

My own daughter, Sharon, brought this home to me when she was about four. I had just mentioned that Aunt Sophia hadn't any children of her own. Sharon countered, "What about Bubby? Isn't Bubby Aunt Sophia's child?"

Sophia

Sharon's misperception made me rethink a relationship I had accepted for years. I could understand her four year old logic. After all, Bubby was shorter than Aunt Sophia, and seemed timid and frail. Aunt Sophia, who was *zoftig* and vivacious, *appeared* to be the caregiver.

"Ma, did you take your pill? Ma, you want a sweater?"

What wasn't obvious to a child was the degree to which Aunt Sophia depended on Bubby. "What should I do, Ma? Ma? What should I do?"

Aunt Sophia believed that Bubby was a *tzadik;* therefore her wisdom was Divine. We don't think of sainthood as a Jewish concept, but to Aunt Sophia her mother was a saint.

Bubby, on the other hand, depended on Aunt Sophia to defend her against Zady's tyranny, and to guide her safely through what both of them perceived to be the mine field of life. Aunt Sophia acted as Bubby's eyes when she couldn't read, her ears when she couldn't hear, and her mouth when she couldn't express herself in English. Aunt Sophia spent her life interpreting the world to Bubby—and explaining Bubby to the world.

Reel to Real

Remember the old song, *"Love is a Many Splendored Thing"?* In our family, instead of the word Love, substitute Aunt Sophia. She was indeed splendid, to many different people, in many different ways. To Bubby, she was a loving and devoted daughter. To Zady, that quintessential patriarch, she was as Cordelia was to Lear: a thankless child. To Uncle Irvin, she was everything: his beautiful, "wife, mother, sister and mistress all rolled into one." To her siblings, she was exasperating: too manipulative, and controlling, and she spoiled their children rotten. To her nieces and nephews, she was Lady Bountiful, and Glinda, the Good Witch of the North combined. To me, she was pure magic!

Aunt Sophia still remembered what the other grown-ups forgot: how it feels to be a child. No crisis, no matter how overwhelming, (and to Aunt Sophia life itself was a crisis) made her forget that children need a childhood, an emotionally safe place to grow up.

Having Aunt Sophia was like having my own Fairy Godmother. She bought me presents when it wasn't my birthday, brought me ice cream when I was sick, and offered me candy when I hadn't eaten my vegetables ("Have some honey, it's *good* for you!") For a child growing up in a "Doing without makes you a better person!" household, she was a dream come true.

Somehow, she was able to nurture that special part of herself, and keep it separate—for the children. How she managed such a feat, I'll never know. It was nothing short of miraculous given the life she had. From childhood on she had carried huge responsibilities, often missing school when Bubby needed her at home. Cooking, cleaning, working after school and all day Saturdays. Stealing soap and toilet paper from her employer at the Five and Ten. Her father had been laid off, and there was no money for even the basic necessities. She knew it was wrong, but her mother had begged her. What else could a "good" daughter do?

Deeds and medical certificates bear *her* signature. ("Sign here Miss Shapiro, right under your father's X.") Her mother weighed her down with confidences, and mouldy family secrets. She had to remember which things she told to whom or, God Forbid, she might cause a catastrophe.

Yet, let a child walk into the room, and presto! "Jo-Annsky-Pansky!" she'd exclaim, shrugging off her fears, the way she'd shrug off a heavy raincoat as soon as the sun shone through. Her eyes sparkled and she laughed till she jiggled, enchanting us with silly games and delicious rhymes to say. Aunt Sophia made the simplest pastimes special. She could turn a walk in the park into a trip to Oz.

Fiercely, she defended the boundaries of our childhood (along with the boundaries of her own, I suspect). Like a female Lancelot, she rode ahead of us, shielding us against a world gone *meshuga,* and in the 1940's we needed all the shielding we could get.

We were at war. Bulletins jackhammered from the radio; newspaper headlines screamed. **Hitler! Air Strikes! Death!** He was murdering our relatives! That maniac with the crooked mustache. Everyone we knew had someone trapped in Europe. Everyone had *someone* fighting overseas. For us it was Uncle Irvin.

TILL A HUNDRED AND TWENTY YEARS

Those were terrible years, as black and white as the Pathe Newsreels, which assaulted us every Saturday at the matinee. "The Eyes and Ears of the World." Stark, grainy footage imprinting itself forever on the movie screen of my memory. I can still see the images. I don't even have to close my eyes.

Masses of people pump their arms up and down like mechanical soldiers. "Heil Hitler, Heil Hitler," they thunder again and again. A wild eyed man with a fat face and plastered down hair screams back at them. His voice is hoarse, his words rasp against my ear drums. He acts more like an animal than a person—a wild boar charging through the forest, or a crazed stallion beginning to buck. A small black square, its ends lopped off by a razor, is pasted on his quaking upper lip. Is it Charlie Chaplin?

Aunt Sophia lost contact with Bubby's mother and sisters in Russia. Bubby cried all the time now, and couldn't be consoled. My parents, still reverberating from the trauma of The Great Depression, moved with a peculiar kind of stiffness, as if they were unsure of where to place their feet. As if at any time, the ground beneath them might explode.

Then in would march Aunt Sophia. "Kookle-Mookle from da duckle!" she'd exclaim, giving my tummy a playful tweak.

She laughed and sang and joked and before I knew it, I was doing it with her. Aunt Sophia not only gave me permission to play, she wouldn't take no for an answer.

"Let's go downtown, honey, I'll buy you a present. You can have anything you want."

Anything I want? Those were magical words. Lucky for Aunt Sophia, I had modest desires. I remember a little black patent leather purse I coveted, and a tiny handkerchief embroidered with red and blue flowers. Aunt Sophia and Bubby picked me up in a taxi—no sooty, smelly streetcars for us! We'd have lunch at Virginia Dare, a "lady's restaurant," where tables were covered with white linen and everyone put her napkin in her lap. I could order anything I wanted (usually a tuna fish sandwhich), and still get strawberry shortcake, even if I left my crusts.

But when I was away from Aunt Sophia's healing presence, there was no way to turn off the nightmare. Even Hollywood stopped making movies I could escape to, and switched to making movies about the war. How we cheered, the adults right along with the children, as our brave American pilots (Alan Ladd, John Wayne, or Randolph Scott), machine-gunned the "yellow peril" out of the wild blue yonder. How we cried when the enemy got one of "our boys," especially when we thought of the wife and children he'd left behind.

Names like Hirohito, Mussolini, Goering, and Goebbels, slid off my five year old tongue as easily as the names of the Mutant Ninja Turtles slide off my five year old grandson's. Places called Corregidor, Guadalcanal, and Bataan were as familiar to me, in 1943, as Disneyland and Sea World are now to the kids next door.

The sense of impending disaster was almost unbearable. Whole towns were blown away before our eyes. Ordinary families were suddenly homeless: old people like Bubby and Zady, little kids like my cousin Sandy and me. Fear churned in the pit of my stomach. Could our homes be destroyed like those others? Would we become refugees?

The images were relentless and terrifying. Children crying for their parents. Husbands searching for their wives. Sometimes I had to put my head down, and cover my ears so I wouldn't have to hear their cries.

But after dinner on a quiet summer evening, Aunt Sophia would stroll by. "Come on, Shmoogle-Poogle, let's go get some ice cream." Together we walked to Dr. Diener's Drug store. She kept me chatting happily all the way.

"What do you want honey?"

"A vanilla sugar cone."

"You want Jimmies on it?" Jimmies were chocolate sprinkles. "Go ahead. Have Jimmies on it." Then she'd turn to the druggist, "Give her lots of Jimmies. And make sure they're fresh!"

Then suddenly, it seemed, before the war was even over, there was Technicolor! Like in the story of Creation when God said "Let there be light," and there was light. The screen came *alive* with sensuous musicals, shimmering costumes, and sparkling dance floors. Jose Iturbi played a piano made entirely of glass. When Carmen Miranda *Quanta le Gusta*-ed her rainbow ruffles across the dance floor, I found myself shaking my hips and shoulders, and *Quanta le Gusta*-ing too.

In my real world, Aunt Sophia was as life-affirming as Carmen Miranda. When she entered a room, she brought the sun in with her. Not just the light and the warmth, but the *energy*. Her golden hair shimmered, her jewelry glistened, her bright blue dresses (which matched her eyes) whispered when she walked. They felt delectably silky to my fingers; a nice change from *our* sensible cotton and scratchy wool.

Now I realize how worried she must have been; about the Jews being murdered in Europe, about the fate of Bubby's family, and about Uncle Irvin's safety overseas. But nothing was ever allowed to mar our outings. This was her special time with me, and she gave us both a little vacation from THE WAR.

I remember a movie I once saw. It was filmed in black and white, and chronicled the depressing odyssey of Mary Lennox, an orphan who came to live on a bleak Yorkshire moor. About half-way through the movie, with the help of a friend, she discovers a hidden gate. As she enters *The Secret Garden,* the screen bursts magically into color. Suddenly there is *LIFE* in that garden, and that Life eventually gets transmitted to Mary herself.

Aunt Sophia could always turn my black and white world into a secret garden. All she had to do was walk in the front door.

Supper with Aunt Sophia

Nothing lasts forever—even in my family. After ten years of loyal patronage, Aunt Sophia, Uncle Irvin and Bubby switched their alliegiance from Howard Johnson's to an exotic new restaurant called, *The Lotus*. Bubby, who was a master of economical description, renamed it *Di Chinezer,* meaning The Chinese. With a single stroke of her inimitable Yiddish shorthand, she could slice through pretension, and get right to the *emes.*

For Aunt Sophia's purposes, Di Chinezer was in a perfect location. Unlike Howard Johnson's, it was not only close to our house, it was also close to Uncle Morris'. Thus they could while away their afternoons by *The Lotus,* then drop in on one of us—for the evening.

Here's the way it happened every Sunday for the next several years:

Time: Around two p.m.

Place: *The Lotus*

Enter: Uncle Irvin, Aunt Sophia, and Bubby. After shmoozing a little with the receptionist and waitress, trying out several tables, getting answers to all of their menu questions, plus personal recommendations from the chef, and the owners of the restaurant, they order. By three-thirty, Aunt Sophia and Uncle Irvin have put away a large calorie-laden meal. Bubby, who is convinced that at four feet, eleven inches, and one hundred and thirty-three pounds, she resembles the fat lady in the circus, has picked at whatever

Supper with Aunt Sophia

they brought her. "You know my mother," Aunt Sophia confides to the restaurant at large, "she eats like a bird!"

Now that his stomach is full, Uncle Irvin lights up a cigarette, orders his second cup of coffee, and spreads out with the Sunday paper. Bubby and Aunt Sophia circulate among their fellow diners, and *kibbitz* with the regulars.

About four, they return to the table for a *nosh*. Uncle Irvin orders another cup of coffee and lights another cigarette. Relaxing over their afternoon snack, they chat with the harried waitresses and busboys who attempt to hurry by.

Five p.m.: Aunt Sophia becomes restless. It's time for Phase II. Squeezing herself out of the Naugahyde booth, she trips down the long corridor to the public phone, and calls Uncle Morris or my mother.

Aunt Sophia: "We're at *The Lotus*. It's nice and warm here." (In the summer, substitute cool.) "Why don't you all come on over?"

I don't know about Uncle Morris, but visiting her family in restaurants is not my mother's idea of a good time. It isn't that she doesn't love them, it's just that whenever she's with them, she loses control of her life.

Mother: "We can't come, Soph. We're busy! We have work to do around the house."

If that's the best Mother can come up with, then our fate is sealed. If we can't come to The Family, The Family will most assuredly come to us.

Aunt Sophia, sensing resistance, switches tactics. Using her sweetest, most conciliatory tone, she resumes. "Is it all right if we come over *there* for a while? Mommy wants to see the children."

Mother hesitates for a fraction of a millisecond, and Aunt Sophia produces the zinger. "Poor thing," she mourns. "Mommy suffers so. The only pleasure she has is seeing the children."

Though mortally wounded Mother rallies, but her voice lacks its previous authority. "Everybody's busy, Soph. No one can entertain you."

Aunt Sophia, knowing victory is hers, reassures her. "We won't even be in the way, we'll just sit for awhile. You won't even know we're there."

Mother knows when she's beaten. Between gritted teeth she asks, "What time are you coming?"

"In a little while." Aunt Sophia doesn't like to be too specific.

Mother tries again. "Would you like to come for dinner?"

"We're not even hungry; we just had a big meal. We'll see you later." And before Mother can extract any more information, Aunt Sophia hangs up.

It is now six p.m. Our family is just sitting down to the table. The bell rings. "I knew it!" Mother grumbles, rolling her eyes in exasperation. Muttering bitter imprecations, she stalks to the door.

There, in her plain black coat, clutching her plain black bag stands Bubby. She looks like an orphan who has even been rejected by The Home. Except for the Parkinson's tremor of her head and right arm, she is motionless. Her aspect is calm, but her expression speaks volumes. Translating loosely from the Yiddish, I read: *I'm sorry for the intrusion. Sophia and Irvin brought me. It was not my idea.* Mother hastens to assure Bubby she is welcome. Only then will Bubby advance farther into the room.

Behind Bubby looms Aunt Sophia. Although she is only three inches taller, she appears Amazonian next to Bubby's pale fragility. Despite being encased in a voluminous green coat, she is as voluptuous as Botticelli's Venus. The long white strands of fur on her collar sway gently against the soft curve of her rouged cheek as she moves majestically toward me. Her hair shines like spun gold, and her blue eyes, like her earrings, twinkle merrily.

Supper with Aunt Sophia

"Hi Kit, hi Mary. How's my Shmoogle—Poogle?" she asks tweaking my belly with a twist of her manicured finger.

Uncle Irvin, who's been waiting, as usual, for Aunt Sophia to move, sweeps in looking crisp and freshly laundered. Beaming at my mother, he swoops down and plants a perfunctory kiss on her disaproving lips. "Hi Mary." Then he grins at me. "How ya doin, Doc?" He grabs me in a bone-crushing embrace, and kisses me soundly. "On the cheek Irv, on the cheek!" Mother reminds him. She is convinced that kissing on the lips spreads germs.

After distributing generous hugs and juicey kisses, Aunt Sophia propels her corseted body straight to the couch. There is a special spot on the floor where she always deposits her cavernous purse. Inside is everything she or Bubby might possibly require, in this world or the next. In addition to keys, money and cosmetics, she carries an assortment of bills, receipts and letters, all neatly folded and stacked in alphabetical order. If she needed to, she could put her finger on any item at a moment's notice, but Aunt Sophia never moves that fast.

Next to her portable filing cabinet, she places the large brown grocery sack containing all of Bubby's medications. Aunt Sophia won't go anywhere without that grocery sack. It is like the President's Black Box. On top of the pills she has carefully folded two thick sweaters—ammunition for her war of attrition against my father. They disagree over just how warm it should be in our house. Daddy insists that anything above 68° is wasteful. Even in the dead of winter. Aunt Sophia argues that 80° should be the absolute minimum, and Bubby agrees.

"Mommy says the reason the children get sick is because *you* keep the house so cold!" Aunt Sophia constantly admonishes my father. But when Daddy feels challenged, he can be just as stubborn as she is. At some point in this ongoing argument, Aunt Sophia realized she had met her match. Now instead of wasting time and breath in useless arguing, she simply takes a different tack. As soon as Mother takes their coats, Aunt Sophia and Bubby begin to shiver.

"Boy, it's some *cold* in here," Aunt Sophia exclaims. "Ma!" she bellows to Bubby, who is hard-of-hearing, *"Du bist kalt?"*

Bubby nods, a pathetic look on her long suffering face. Aunt Sophia fumbles with the grocery sack, and after much rattling of paper (the louder the better to impress my father), she extracts the twin sweaters. She unbuttons Bubby's, and helps her on with it. "Are you warm enough, Ma?" she shouts. Bubby shakes her head, and pulls her sweater closer about her. Daddy pretends he is as hard-of-hearing as Bubby.

Aunt Sophia stows Bubby on the couch. "Are you all right, Ma?" she asks several times. Each time Bubby nods yes.

Now that the Preliminaries are out of the way, Aunt Sophia slides smoothly into Getting Acclimated. Wandering through the house, she rakes each room with the x-ray eye of an experienced customs inspector. She reads our mail, opens our drawers, and comments on everything.

"Oh, look at this—is it new, Mary? When did you get it? How much did you pay? Look Irv, look what Mary got. *Ma! Gib a kick."*

Mother interrupts Aunt Sophia's meanderings. "We're just about to eat Soph. Would you like to sit down?"

"Oh, I didn't *know* you were eating. Go ahead, eat!" Aunt Sophia becomes truly concerned over anyone being separated from his food.

Wearily, Mother repeats the invitation. She knows it's part of the ritual. "Are you *sure* you won't join us?" But this time she speaks through clenched teeth.

Aunt Sophia waves an airy hand of dismissal. "No thanks, we just ate. We won't even bother you. We'll just watch."

Mother bulges her eyes, and glances heavenwards. I can read her lips as she mouths, "God in heaven, give me strength!"

Mother, Daddy, Gischa, Larry, and I sit down and start eating.

Uncle Irvin lights a cigarette and paces the room, questioning Daddy about his views on the latest government scandal. Bubby perches on the edge of the couch, silently shrinking into her thick pink sweater. Aunt Sophia peramblates around the table and comments on the food.

"Gee, everything looks so *good*, Mary. What kind of fish is that?" Without listening to the answer she continues. "Where did you buy it? Gee, it looks delicious. How do you cook it? Boy, it sure looks good. I bet Mommy would like a piece of fish like that. Do you think it would hurt her, Mary? I wonder if she'll eat it.

"Ma! Bist hingerick?"

Bubby nods yes.

"Ma! Vilst a schtikelle fish? Mary gemacht. Siz azay shane!"

Bubby nods again.

"Kim a hair, Ma, zitsin-du."

Bubby gets up from the sofa, turns and smooths away the impression her body has left on the cushion. Timidly, she approaches the table.

"Kit!" Mother shouts, breaking into his impassioned discussion with Uncle Irvin. "Get my mother a chair."

Daddy jumps up, crashes into the table, and fetches a chair. Mother brings an extra place setting. Bubby protests. She is too much trouble. She is certain we don't have enough. Who is she to take food out of the mouths of her grandchildren?

"Come on Bubby, come and sit with us," we chorus.

Head lowered like a chastened servant, she accepts the chair placed next to mine. Patting me on the arm, she smiles conspiratorily, and hands me a wrinkled paper bag. "For you Jo-Vennala, and Gischa and Lar'n."

"Thank you, Bubby." I peek inside. The bag is filled with after-dinner mints. I look at my grandmother.

"From di Chinezer," she explains.

She must have emptied the entire dish of after dinner mints that the restaurant keeps by the cash register.

"Bubby," I remind her, "You're only supposed to take one or two."

She shrugs her shoulders. "Dey got plenna money."

Aunt Sophia piles food on Bubby's empty plate. "Look at her, poor thing, she's so thin, she eats like a bird! *Ma! Vilst a bissel lucshon? A bissel brait? Ess, Ma, ess!*"

"Soph," says my mother in a strangled voice, "would *you* like to eat something?"

"Who, me? No. I'm not even hungry. That koogle looks wonderful. Did you make it, Mary?"

Aunt Sophia was so terrified of cooking, she was always amazed at anyone else's culinary success.

"Come on, Aunt Sophia, sit down and eat with us," we beg. "Yeah. Come on Aunt Sophia."

Bubby sits quietly eating. She could be invisible if not for the stuttering clink of her metal fork against her china plate. She leans her wrist against the edge of the table in a vain effort to control her palsied arm.

"I'm telling you, Kit, they're all a bunch of crooks!" yells Uncle Irvin, still pacing in the living room.

" Aw, you don't know what you're talking about Irv," shoots back my father.

Their arguing provides a continuous counterpoint to the progress of the meal.

"Maybe I'll just have a little taste of that koogle, Mary," Aunt Sophia offers, as if she only wants to do my mother a favor.

Supper with Aunt Sophia

Somebody brings another chair. We all shift over making room for Aunt Sophia. Mother brings another plate. Aunt Sophia helps herself to a tiny piece of koogle.

"Mmmm, this is delicious! Mary. Mommy puts a little more sugar, but it's delicious. Here honey, (to my sister) take some koogle. It's delicious!"

"I have some, Aunt Sophia."

"Have some *more;* it's really *good!* How about you, honey?"

"I already have some, Aunt Sophia."

"How about you, Kit?—Kit! Try some koogle."

"I got some, Soph."

"Irv, you should taste this koogle! Delicious!"

Aunt Sophia digs in with gusto, devouring fish, bread, a little from every dish on the table. As she tastes each course she repeats, "This food is really delicious—you should taste some!" To which we all reply, "We have some Aunt Sophia."

Bubby has lost interest in the fish. She sits and stares into the far distance.

Uncle Irvin and Daddy finish politicians and move on to building contractors.

Mother gets up to make the tea and coffee. Gish and I clear the table. Aunt Sophia, now on her umpteenth helping, laughs and talks as she chews, waving her fork with gay abandon.

Uncle Irvin joins us for dessert and coffee. Everyone "ohhhs" and "ahhhhs" as the strudel Daddy bought from Silber's is carried to the table. Succulent red cherries burst through the brown latticed crust and ooze onto the plate as Daddy slices into it. Bits of cinnamon-sugar glisten on top.

Daddy stops talking and concentrates on his strudel. With quick deft movements, he separates the forkfuls, and hurls them into his mouth. "Mmmm." He growls with contentment at every bite.

Uncle Irvin gazes dreamily at the smoke from his cigarette and the steam from his coffee as they curl slowly upward and dissipate into the air.

Bubby's cup clank, clank, clanks against her saucer.

Larry and Gischa and I eat quietly, savoring the unexpected sweet.

Mother's shoulders sag, and her pretty face looks rueful. She chews her strudel as if it's a task she must accomplish. Between bites, she takes dejected sips of her tepid tea.

Aunt Sophia's ample chest is liberally sprinkled with strudel crumbs. Her smiling mouth is stained a wine dark red. "Isn't this wonderful?" she demands.

Again she insists that each of us "have another piece of strudel," but everyone declines. Mother indicates it's time to clear the dessert dishes. Gisch gathers the cups and saucers, and I stack the sticky plates. Aunt Sophia helps herself to yet another serving. "I don't know what's the matter with all of you," she declares as we carry our fragile burden into the kitchen. "The whole bunch of you eat like birds!"

Salutations and Signatures

Aunt Sophia held two important positions in The Family: Chief Public Relations Officer, *and* Chairman of Good and Welfare. These positions were not only self-appointed, they were indisputably hers—for life!

She kept track of everything that went on with everybody. Besides calling the relatives several times a day, she was a confirmed and inveterate card sender. Long before greeting cards became big business, Aunt Sophia was already raising Hallmark's profit margin. She not only cared enough to send the very best—she did it often. It was one of her rituals. Whether with cheery get well cards or exhuberant valentines, Aunt Sophia believed in marking occasions.

She took great pleasure in selecting just the right card with just the right message, and she was willing to spend hours accomplishing her goal. Chirpy bluebirds, singing rainbow-colored songs, urged me to "feel better soon." Lacey red valentines implored "Please be Mine." I loved them all.

Especially the birthday cards. For birthdays, Aunt Sophia pulled out all the stops. The cards she sent were always oversized and beautiful—like she was. So what if they cost a little extra? Weren't they for "the children?"

Each one had something unusual: like a clown who danced on a spring, a peek-a-boo door behind which hid a lovable baby animal, or a detachable button that had my exact age painted on it. How did she do that? I wondered.

How did she find a card that knew exactly how old I was? I would wear my button till it fell to pieces. I wanted everyone in the neighborhood to know that *I* was the birthday girl. In my house, children were admonished to be "seen and not heard." It felt good, once in a while, to be special.

Aunt Sophia's cards enchanted me with their magic. Their brilliant colors danced across the page and carried me along with them. My birthday number sparkled, encrusted with the glitter of fairy dust. I caressed the shiny satin bows with my sticky fingers, and blew ever so lightly on the feathery ostrich plumes. The filmy fronds swayed and bent like trees in a raging windstorm. Their silken whisper tickled my tender skin.

Those cards were a feast for my soul, and every year she sent two.

"To a Wonderful Grandaughter," proclaimed one.

"To a Special Niece," sang the other. Scrawled across the tops of both cards was "Dear Shmoogle-Poogle." Across the bottoms, "Love and XOXOXOXOXO till a hundred and twenty years!" One was signed Bubby and Zady, the other Aunt Sophia and Uncle Irvin. Since neither Zady nor Bubby could write, Aunt Sophia was also the Family Scribe.

Those were the early years, when Bubby cooked her wonderful food, cleaned the house till it squeaked, and nurtured her growing family. With three paychecks coming in, there was money for extras like dinners in fancy restaurants, vacations in Atlantic City, and lots of expensive presents for the children.

Then Bubby got sick and could no longer be the *balabusta*. Aunt Sophia developed an eye problem and had to quit her job. Now they were down one pay check, but their expenses kept going up. Aunt Sophia tried to keep Bubby busy and entertained. They must have spent a fortune on taxis, not to mention restaurants, since Aunt Sophia was afraid to cook. In addition, they had to pay someone to do the cleaning.

Before long the DMV took away Zady's license. They said he was too old to teach driving anymore. Now they were down two paychecks and the medical expenses kept rising. That was the year "Dear Jo-Ann," became the salutation, and the signature was "Love XOXOXOXO till a hundred and twenty years! Aunt Sophia, Uncle Irvin, Bubby and Zady." All four names on one card.

As the years went by, life got tougher and tougher for Aunt Sophia. Yet, every year my card arrived on time. Each one was exceptionally beautiful; graced by masses of pastel flowers and glittery with diaphanous butterflies and plump bees. The message printed inside always embarrassed me—there were too many superlatives, and she would underline each one.

In May, 1966, came another big change. "Happy Birthday, honey. Love and XOXOXOXO, till a hundred and twenty years! Aunt Sophia, Uncle Irvin, and Bubby." How odd the signature looked. Unsymmetrical. Exposed. *Vulnerable*. Never before had Aunt Sophia sent a card without Zady's name on it. Even when they'd been at the height of their war! It had taken death to change that ritual.

Five years later came another big change. "Love and XOXOXO, till a hundred and twenty years. Aunt Sophia and Uncle Irvin." We were down to two. On the back was a note from Aunt Sophia assuring me that even in heaven, Bubby wished me well on my birthday. How painful it must have been for her to stop writing Bubby's name after thirty-two years! It was terrible for me not to read it—a continual reminder of our loss. As if we needed one.

In 1975, Uncle Irvin developed lung cancer. Uncle Irvin! Her anchor! Especially after Bubby died. Over the next two years she spent hours with him in the hospital, questioning his doctors, manipulating the nurses, *keeping him alive*.

"Uncle Irvin doesn't feel so good, honey," she'd say in her letters. "You know how it is." She was so terrified of losing him, she couldn't bring herself to name his disease. "Uncle Irvin sends a big kiss to you and Stanley and the children. Pray for him, honey, I wish he'll be well."

The tightly woven fabric of Aunt Sophia's life was unraveling, but she still managed to send my cards on time. "Loving Thoughts for a Special Niece," said the first year's. "Birthday Wishes for the Birthday Girl," said the next. Each was signed "Love and XOXOXO, till a hundred and twenty years! Aunt Sophia and Uncle Irvin."

Then Uncle Irvin died on Valentine's Day, 1977. The bitter irony wasn't lost on Aunt Sophia. After thirty-seven years of marriage, she had lost her sweetheart, her companion, her friend. Everyone said, "Sophia's strong, but she'll never survive this one." Yet when May rolled around, she sent my card as usual. "Happy Birthday to a Dear Niece. Love and kisses, Aunt Sophia." We were down to one.

With Uncle Irvin gone, Aunt Sophia's finances became very limited. She complained of severe pain in her back, her legs, and her head. Now she "ran to the doctor" for herself, not for Bubby or Uncle Irvin. Yet my special cards continued to arrive, year after year. Aunt Sophia had a code and "the children," whether adult now or not, were always her top priority.

Then one icy winter's day, she fell and broke her hip. When May 23rd arrived there was no card from Aunt Sophia. I wasn't surprised. I knew she was incapacitated. But six months later, my card did arrive, with a heartfelt message scribbled across the bottom. "Please forgive me, honey, for missing your birthday."

After her accident, Aunt Sophia became less and less mobile. Her world shrank to the size of her tiny apartment. She wrote, "I get so lonely. I talk to the walls, but if they answered me, I would be frightened!"

She lost interest in herself and gained so much weight she could no longer fit in her dresses. She refused to wear anything we bought her, prefering hand-me-down pants suits inherited from dead relatives. She stopped wearing make-up and going to the beauty shop. Her once golden hair became white. She must have seen the surprise on my face when I saw her.

"Who do I have to stay blonde for?" she demanded, a note of resigned bitterness in her voice .

Aunt Sophia may have lost interest in herself, but she never lost interest in her "children." Year after year she sent cards.

In December, 1988, Aunt Sophia died very suddenly. One day she was there, and the next day she wasn't. There will be no more cards signed, "Love and kisses till a hundred and twenty years, Aunt Sophia."

Those cards were like her life. From fullness and plenty they diminished over time, bit by bit—till there was nothing left. Except the memories.

Endings—and Beginnings

The Family's reaction to change was always predictable—stout denial. Their attitude was: if you don't acknowledge it, it won't happen. This was how they defended themselves against a reality they understood only too well: life *is* change—full of endings and beginnings which are often too painful to accept.

When Zady died in 1965, he changed the shape of The Family constellation forever. He had reduced their solidity as a quartet to the unwieldy wobble of a trio. They were taken by surprise, and thrown off balance.

We were sad to lose Zady, but we were also relieved, and a little guilty. He had been a contentious force in our family for so long. Maybe now we could enjoy a little peace and quiet.

But we forgot with whom we were dealing. Toward the end of his life, when he hadn't earned a living for so long, and had become so physically limited, we had relegated him to Minor Character in the Shapiro Family drama. We were foolish enough to believe that he had surrendered the formidable power he'd once commanded. Were we wrong!

Just as the moon exerts an enormous pull on the tides although it appears pale in comparison to the sun, Zady exerted a similar power in the Family, even though Aunt Sophia appeared to outshine him. He had been the immovable force against which all the others had reacted. Without him to richochet off, they became confused and lost. Zady had provided their focus. As their acknowledged enemy, he had been both visible and familiar. They'd spent years devising strategies to outsmart him, and suddenly—he was gone.

They decided to sell the house on Oakley Avenue. The neighborhood had deteriorated, as had the house, and they could no longer afford to repair it. Aunt Sophia complained that the stairs were bad for her back and for Bubby's heart.

Practical considerations are one thing. Abandoning a house that's been the center of your life for fifty years is quite another. How do you sever your emotional life line without bleeding to death? What would they do with the memories?

Their lives had been filled with hard times, but this must have been one of the hardest. Like relinquishing a life preserver in forty feet of water when you know you can't swim. It was the end of an era.

The house sold in the summer of 1967 and Aunt Sophia began preparations for the move. This meant combing through the combined possessions of four people who had not thrown anything away for half a century. Anyone would have been daunted by such a formidable task.

I flew in from Rochester to see them and to say goodbye to the house on Oakley Avenue for the last time.

As I stepped off the plane the heat beat against me like a hammer. The humidity pressed me down against the ground.

I called as soon as I got settled. "I'm here, Aunt Sophia. I made it safe and sound."

"Where are you honey?" She sounded far away, as if I were calling from New York.

"At Mother's. When can I come?"

Silence.

"Aunt Sophia? I can't wait to see you. When can I come?"

"I want to see you too, honey, you know I'd love to see you, but it's not a good time." Her voice kept fading into the distance, as if she were floating away.

"Well, when is a good time?"

"How's Stanley—and the children?"

"They're fine, Aunt Sophia. I came all the way from Rochester. I want to see you!"

"You don't understand, honey, it's a big mess here."

"I don't care about the mess. Maybe I can help."

"Thank you, honey, thank you, but you can't do it. We'll see you when you come next time."

"I'm coming, Aunt Sophia, I'll be there in a little while."

Remembering Aunt Sophia's daily rituals, I timed my arrival for after lunch. She was still in her nightgown, her hair all *tzpottled,* and her face, without make-up, like a ghost's. Aunt Sophia looked strained, as if something was squeezing her tightly and she was afraid she'd pop.

Stuff was everywhere. Wherever I looked there were stacks of clothes and crockery, and who-knew-what.

"See? I told you honey. You shouldn't have come."

Perspiration ran and dribbled down her neck pasting her nylon bodice against her skin in large wet patches. She sleepwalked around the piles, moving from the vestibule through the hallway. Back and forth she wandered, circling one pile, and then another.

"Whew! It's some hot, isn't it honey?" She was trying to cool her dripping face with a flapping hand.

"It sure is, Aunt Sophia." I felt so sorry for her.

Bubby, forbidden to work because of her heart, stood on the sidelines looking owlish. Not being able to help was a terrible punishment for her. Worse. Seeing her daughter so distraught broke her heart. She watched Aunt Sophia's meanderings with eyes full of pity. For the first time in my life, she was hardly aware that I was there.

Since Aunt Sophia rejected all my well-meant suggestions, I moved on through the cluttered hallway to the breakfast room. This was where Bubby had served us her wonderful Sabbath dinners, where Aunt Sophia and Zady had battled for ascendancy, and where important family decisions had been made. Even now, the breakfast room was where The Family gathered, and where they entertained on those now rare occasions that they had a guest.

The first thing I saw was Zady's armchair. Empty. I felt my heart contract. Without his reassuring bulk it was just a piece of furniture, lifeless and unfamiliar. Every corner of the room awakened a memory. I had spent so much time in this house. So much of my childhood belonged to it.

There was the window Bubby almost fell out of in her passion to *vanquish the shmutz*. And the footstool! Uncle Morris built that in 1927 so Bubby could reach the storage cabinet. It still squatted under the drain board, ready for Bubby to help me up on it as she had when I had been too little to reach the kitchen sink. I tested it with my foot. Still solid as it ever was, but the paint was worn. In some places I could see the naked wood beneath.

I peeked into Zady's bedroom. Still dark and sinister. Gish and I had always thought of it as Zady's lair.

Back-tracking through the hallway, and around Aunt Sophia, I wandered into the sun "poller." Either it should have been built on the *south* side of the house, or it should have been given another name. It was so cold nobody but Zady would sit in it. He listened to *Di Yiddishe Radio Shtunde* in there.

Sometimes, as a child, I liked to listen with him. I'd sit on the floor in front of him with my ear pushed against the speaker, and wonder, *How do they fit such big people into such a little cabinet?*

To the left of the sun parlor was the living room. All the "good" things were displayed in there: Bubby's pink silk Victorian couch that nobody ever sat on, the tables that were so highly polished I could see myself looking sadly back, and the ornate porcelain lamps with their fluted shades, still wearing their plastic covers. Each piece sat where it had sat forever. I could have found my way around that room in the dark.

I started up the steps.

"Wait a minute honey, I'll go with you. There's something I want you to see." Aunt Sophia completed the circle she had started, and joined me on the stairs. As we passed the telephone on the other side of the bannister, a memory flashed.

"Remember the night that Larry was born, Aunt Sophia?"

"Do I! You and Gischa were so *coxited* you couldn't even sleep."

"We were excited? What about you and Uncle Irvin? Everytime the phone rang, he flew down these stairs so fast his feet never touched a single step."

Aunt Sophia mopped her face, and chuckled to herself. "That little monkey, Larry. He had us some worried. We were waiting so long!"

We strolled through the upstairs bedrooms. Aunt Sophia continued to point things out. "Here, honey, you want these dishes? They're brand new. I got them when I was married. I never used them. They've been in the basement all these years. Take 'em, honey, please."

"I don't need them, Aunt Sophia. Besides, I can't carry much on the plane."

Again and again she offered, and again and again I declined.

As she talked, my eyes panned the familiar rooms like a movie camera, burning the familiar images into my brain.

Endings and Beginnings

I watched myself going through the motions with her. I must have seemed so calm on the surface, so detached. Then what was that pounding against my insides? As if someone kept punching, and twisting my gut. Memory after bittersweet memory bombarded me, stacking up inside me like books on a warehouse floor.

We entered Aunt Sophia's bedroom. "Here, honey. I know you always loved it. This is for you." She was pointing to the "cuckoo" clock.

It was a tiny little thing, no bigger than the palm of my hand. Instead of a single cuckoo it had two little lovebirds facing each other. As the pendulum moved, the birds bent forward and "kissed." It had been one of her wedding presents and had been hanging on that wall since 1940, when I was two.

When I was a child, Aunt Sophia inaugurated a ritual. Whenever I came for a visit, (which was often since I lived down the street) she held me up to see the birdies. Kiss-kiss, kiss-kiss, kiss-kiss. I was enchanted! I could tell Aunt Sophia enjoyed it too. She cuddled me against her soft, sweet smelling flesh and I felt perfect contentment. I was not only safe, I was surrounded by love.

Aunt Sophia could turn an ordinary clock into an adventure. Maybe because the child in her was never far away. She had the body of a grown-up, but we weren't fooled. She was really one of us; that's why we loved her so.

Many years later she would introduce my own young daughters to the ritual. Each time we came to visit, Aunt Sophia held them up and each was enchanted by the wonderful clock.

This was the first time I had seen the "cuckoo" for years. Most of our recent visits had been in restaurants or at my mother's.

As I stared at the clock, my stomach tightened. Suddenly I understood what it symbolized. Predictability.

Like the rock solid predictability of life in that house, which translated for me into a feeling of sanctuary. Love. As expressed between the real lovebirds in my life, Aunt Sophia and Uncle Irvin. And Aunt Sophia herself, and the absolute delight I took in her company.

"It's broken, honey. I'm sorry. It doesn't work anymore. When I wind it up, nothing happens."

Gently, I flicked the delicate pendulum with my fingertip. As it swung from side to side, the lovebirds leaned toward each other and kissed.

"It's all right, Aunt Sophia, I'll get it fixed," I promised. "I love that clock."

She lifted it off the wall, and laid it carefully in my outstretched hand. "Take good care of it, honey. And don't lose the key!" she admonished.

I don't remember the rest of the visit. I only remember the incredible sense of heaviness, dark and jagged, massing inside me like clouds massing before a deluge.

When I returned to Rochester, the humidity was as intense as it had been in Baltimore. My skin seemed to shrink against my bones. I could hardly stand the weight. I moved through the house on legs that felt like tree stumps: unpacking, doing laundry, answering questions for Stanley and the girls. The clock wasn't ticking, but I was. Like a walking time bomb, I was pregnant with my load of unexpressed grief.

After carefully unwrapping my precious heirloom, I handed it to Stanley.

"Do you think you could fix it?"

He turned it over. "Let me try."

"I don't want *anything* to happen to it. Please, be careful!"

"I know," he assured me. "I will."

I lay on the couch, watching him *potshky* with it. I felt frozen, numb and stiff as a cadaver, yet inside I felt bruised.

No sounds floated in through the open living room windows. The girls were quietly sleeping upstairs.

All of a sudden, **"sprong!"** Clock pieces exploded in every direction. Sprong! An answering explosion within me. "Noooooooo!" Deep, gut-wrenching sobs screamed out of me. I wept with the abandon I had wept with as a child. I was finally grieving—for Zady, for what was left of The Family, and for a treasured time I had lost for good. I cried as though I'd never finish crying. It was my *life* that had just been shattered—not just a "cuckoo" clock.

Stanley let me cry. He knew I was inconsolable. Without a word he gathered up the pieces and began to reassemble the clock.

Finally the cataclysm passed.

"It's all right now, see?" he showed me. "It'll be all right. I'm *sure* a clock-maker can fix it."

I nodded, too exhausted to speak. But I felt cleansed, the way the air feels after a violent thunder storm. Maybe it *would* be all right.

The clock was repaired and continued to run for many years. Wherever we moved, we took it with us. When we built a vacation house on Cape Cod, we filled it with all our most cherished possessions. Aunt Sophia's lovebirds had the place of honor on the living room wall. As soon as we walked in the door, I wound that clock. Once the little birds were kissing, I knew we were home.

Aunt Sophia is gone now. But her little clock sits on the wall in my writing room, where I look at it every day. It no longer runs because its parts are worn out, and can no longer be replaced. But if I gently flick the pendulum with the tip of my index finger, the lovebirds still kiss—now for my three grandsons.

She Also Serves who Only Stands and Waits

Aunt Sophia would never have been mistaken for a famous explorer—unless the territory to be explored was good food. Then she was a regular Columbus. A new restaurant opening in Baltimore beckoned to Aunt Sophia the way a new route to the Orient beckoned to the discoverers of the New World. If she found the food tasty, and the staff sympathetic, she brought Bubby. If Bubby agreed that the place was also clean enough, she gave her nod of approval—and they moved in.

That's how I came to be at *Wolfie's,* one Saturday evening. I was in town on one of my in-and-out visits, but Aunt Sophia insisted I join them to eat. Uncle Irvin had not yet arrived when I got there, but I couldn't miss Aunt Sophia. Her golden-haired, green-coated ship of state had stalled in the middle of the main aisle. Feet wide apart, arms akimbo, she was a latter day Isabella, claiming this new territory as her own.

Bubby, standing on the side in her plain black coat, looked a little worn, as though she'd just disembarked from steerage. She was deep in conversation with an elderly waitress. The waitress' hand rested lovingly on Bubby's shoulder as she gazed deep into the sadness of Bubby's round eyes. As Bubby talked the woman nodded and, with the regularity of a metronome, clucked her tongue.

She also Serves

Aunt Sophia expanded with pleasure the minute she saw me. "Hi, honey; how are you? How was your trip?"

"Mmmmmfffh," I said, from the interior of my aunt's generous bosom. She had already enveloped me in one of her fur-collared shmoogle-poogle hugs.

Then, over my shoulder, she hollered, "Ma! Ma! Look who's here!"

Bubby glanced up, and smiled when she saw me. *Oy, an angel dropped down from heaven to see me!* I read in her adoring face.

"Hi, Bubby," I said, stooping to hug and kiss her. Without a word, she took my hand, cradled it as if it were some priceless treasure, and kissed it again and again. I don't think the *Mashiach* would have gotten a warmer reception.

Aunt Sophia turned to the waitress. "This is my niece, Jo-Annsky-Pansky, who came *all the way from Massachusetts"* (as though Massachusetts was in another galaxy, and I had come all this distance just to eat at Wolfie's.) In her own subtle way, Aunt Sophia was signaling the waitress that this was a special occasion and would require special attention. After all, beloved relatives do not descend from the wilds of Massachusetts everyday.

"This is Shirley, honey," Aunt Sophia explained, indicating the waitress. "She takes very good care of us, don't you Shirley?"

Shirley beamed. "And they're a pleasure to take care of, I'm sure!"

Now it was Aunt Sophia's turn to beam. Marching over to a table, she pulled out a chair with an elaborate flourish. "Sit down, honey, sit down. The food here is wonderful, you'll enjoy it. Order *whatever* you want."

I sat down. Bubby and Shirley resumed their conversation. Aunt Sophia bustled over to the waitress' station and procured a paper place mat, a napkin, and a place setting. Just as she was about to arrange them before me, she spied *a bisele schmutz*.

"Here, honey, hold these a minute, I'll be right back." Off she hurried to the waitress' station.

Maybe hurried isn't exactly the right word. Aunt Sophia was more like a bowl of pudding. It wiggles a lot if you move it, but it doesn't actually *go* anywhere.

Bubby and Shirley, oblivious of everything else, continued their conversation. Aunt Sophia returned with a wet *shmata* and attacked the *shmutz*.

"Let me do it. I can do it, Aunt Sophia."

"No, honey. You're my guest." She pushed the *shmata* around and around the table. When she was finally satisfied, she set my place.

Aunt Sophia unconsciously assumed the posture of a waitress. "What would you like, honey? You don't have to wait for Uncle Irvin. I know you're hungry. Tell me what you want."

I shrugged. "I don't really know, Aunt Sophia. I haven't seen a menu."

Aunt Sophia looked around for Shirley, but she and Bubby had just finished the destruction of the Second Temple, and were moving toward the Exile. Before I could stop her, Aunt Sophia was off again.

"Here, honey," she said, returning with a menu the size of the Baltimore telephone directory. "Take your time. Everything is good."

I started reading.

"Are you thirsty, honey? You want some water?"

Without waiting for an answer, she moved away. This time she returned proudly bearing a tall glass of sparkling water. "Drink some, honey, it's good for you. It's fresh," she assured me as I hesitated.

Obediently I sipped the water I didn't really want. It was easier than arguing. Nobody ever won an argument

She also Serves

with Aunt Sophia. I perused the menu. Aunt Sophia stood behind me, reading over my shoulder—out loud.

"How about the whitefish, honey? Bubby likes the whitefish."

"I don't feel like whitefish, Aunt Sophia."

"The chicken salad is delicious! Try the chicken salad."

Clearly she was on intimate terms with most of the offerings.

About the time I made my decision, Bubby and Shirley finished talking. Aunt Sophia gave Shirley my order. "She'll have the brisket, honey, but make sure it's fresh. Is it fresh? Tell them in the kitchen it's for my niece, Jo-Ann. Tell them she came all the way from Massachusetts, hear?"

Then turning to me, "What else, honey, what else?"

"That's enough, Aunt Sophia, just the brisket sandwich."

"That's all? You call that a dinner? That's not enough. Have something else. The chopped liver is wonderful."

"No thank you, Aunt Sophia. Just the brisket."

"How about some soup; the matzo ball is good."

"Just the brisket, Aunt Sophia."

"No wonder you're so thin, you eat like a bird. She eats like a bird," Aunt Sophia confided to Shirley. "Well, save some room for dessert. They have good parfaits here." Aunt Sophia adored parfaits.

Finally, she dispatched Shirley to the kitchen for my dinner. Then she turned to Bubby.

"Here, Ma. *Zitsn-du*." Aunt Sophia helped Bubby out of her coat, settled her into her chair, and went off to find the coat rack. On her way back to the table she stopped at her old haunt, the waitress' station, and returned with a place setting for her mother. As she laid down the knife, fork, and spoon Bubby raised each piece for closer inspection. "It's clean, Ma, it's clean!" Aunt Sophia insisted.

Bubby raked the silver with her special *shmutz* detecting radar. The spoon and the fork passed muster. The knife she gravely handed back. Aunt Sophia laughed, and went for a "fresh" knife.

Eventually she returned, huffing and puffing from her unusual exertions. She surveyed her handiwork. Something was missing, but what? As she concentrated, I watched my favorite crease pucker her lovely brow. Suddenly, the mists cleared. Aha!

"Vilst a bisele vasser, Ma?" Aunt Sophia bellowed.

Bubby shrugged.

She was off again.

By the time my dinner arrived, she was back.

"Is it good, honey; do you like it?"

I had just taken my first bite.

"It's delicious, Aunt Sophia, thank you," I managed with a full mouth.

Aunt Sophia's eyes lit up, and her shoulders relaxed. "See, I told you the food is good here," she reminded, with a matching I-told-you-so smile.

She thought for a moment, then added with a look of pleased triumph, "What I like though...is that the service is so nice!"

Always Leave them Laughing

Dear Aunt Sophia,
Stanley and I are coming to Baltimore at the end of the month, and we want very much to see you. We're flying in from San Diego on Friday, and would like to take you out to lunch on Sunday. This is one of those whirlwind visits, so our time will be very tight. Please be ready at 2 PM <u>sharp</u>. I love you and I can't wait to see you!
Love, XXXX
Jo-Ann

It had been five years since I'd seen Aunt Sophia, but we were finally going home! We kept in touch through letters and phone calls, but her answers came less and less frequently, and when she did write she seemed distracted and sad. Mostly she talked about Bubby and Uncle Irvin: how much she missed them, and how hopeless she felt.

She was afraid to go out by herself since her accident, yet she hated feeling imprisoned at home. Whenever I called, she let the phone ring forever. Then I'd hear, "Helloooh?" so faint and querulous I could hardly believe it was she. The flatness in her voice implied, there's no sense rushing to answer—it couldn't *possibly* be for me.

"How does she spend her time?" I asked my sister, on one of our twice-monthly marathon calls.

"Oh," said Gischa, with a *tone* in her voice, "she finds a way!"

"Like what?" I insisted.

"Like rearranging hangers in Bubby's closet. All of Bubby's clothes are still there. Even her shoes. You know, the ones from Bubby's bunions? Aunt Sophia lines them up in perfect rows along the floor."

"My God, Gish. Bubby's been dead for eighteen years!"

"I know."

"I'm afraid to ask what she does with the hangers."

"Oh, that's simple. She measures to see if they're the same distance apart."

I could *see* Aunt Sophia standing there in Bubby's closet. I watched the crease deepen into a comma between the bridge of her nose and her right eye.

"And that's not the worst of it," Gischa interrupted. "When she escorted me to the bathroom? Like I didn't *know* where the bathroom was? There were *two* towels on the rack."

"So?"

" 'Don't use that one, honey,' she tells me. 'It's Uncle Irvin's.' As if she really expects him to come back."

"Oy, Gish, I feel so terrible!"

"I know. But what can we do?"

A few months later, Larry sent me a clipping from the Baltimore Sun. *Who is that fat old woman with the cane?* I scanned the article and deciphered a scribbled footnote in the margin: "The one in the pink dress is Aunt Sophia." *No!* I forced myself to look again—at the swollen body in the rumpled house dress, the emptiness in the moon-like face, the *tzpottled* hair.

Dear God, this couldn't be Aunt Sophia ...

***

Always Leave them Laughing

All the way from California, I worried. Suppose she really looked like that picture? Suppose she wasn't my old Aunt Sophia anymore?

The minute we pulled into the driveway, I saw her—waving from her living room window, the way I used to do.

"My God," I said to Stanley, "she's actually ready!" Was this the Aunt Sophia who was late for everything, *including* our wedding? The one about whom Mother used to joke, "Whatever time you tell Aunt Sophia you'll pick her up, that's the time she steps into the tub."

Sliding the glass aside, Aunt Sophia called through the open window.

"You said two o'clock on the dot, right? Well, *that's* when I was ready!" A smug smile lit her happy face.

I looked at my watch. 2:15. *Gevalt!* I thought, I'll never live this down.

We hurried inside and hugged her.

"Hi, honey," she burbled, kissing us both. "Are the children all right? When did you get in? I'm so *glad* to see you."

"We're glad to see you too, Aunt Sophia, you look wonderful!"

"Who? A fat old gal like me? So, tell me, honey, what time did you get in?"

"You already asked me that, Aunt Sophia."

"I did? Oh. I guess I'm just coxcited...like Bubby, *aleva shalom*, used to say."

Warmth and energy radiated out of her. Being near her was like basking in the sun.

She bubbled on. "You want something honey? How about some grapes?"

"No thank you, Aunt Sophia. I don't want to spoil my appetite."

"Grapes are *good* for you, honey. How about you Stanley? Want some grapes?"

Now that her attention was focussed on Stanley, I took a minute to check her out. She was definitely heavier, the old green pants suit was more than a little tight. But her hair had been done, and her nails freshly polished.

Thank you God, for keeping her intact!

We bundled her into the car, which wasn't easy. She collapsed, laughing at herself in the back seat.

"Where do you want to eat Aunt Sophia?"

"Just drive! I'll tell you where to stop."

I winked at my husband. Aunt Sophia had roared back to life!

"You both look wonderful, *ken ahora*. You don't even *look* like grandparents. Turn left at this corner, Stanley. I said left! Are the girls all right? I wish they could come. And that kookle-mookle Maxi, he should live and be well!"

Aunt Sophia talked all the way to the deli. "See, I told you it wasn't far!"

The sign said, *Manny's*.

How does she find these places? Who brings her? Does she have a secret life?

There was no point in asking Aunt Sophia. She never answered questions—she only asked them.

As soon as we had pried her out of the car, she took charge. Ponderous and majestic as the Queen Mary, she swept through the front door. Stanley and I followed humbly behind her, like little tug boats in her wake.

The place was small, and mobbed with elderly Jewish couples. We were at the end of a line that stretched for at least six feet.

Aunt Sophia smiled and nodded to her fellow diners, but she was plotting something; I recognized the look. Catching the hostess' eye, she waved and shouted, "HERE ARE MY NIECE AND NEPHEW WHO CAME ALL THE

WAY FROM *CANADA!*" The hostess smiled vaguely, then turned back to her list. Stanley flashed me a raised eyebrow. *Canada?* I shrugged. *Don't ask!* I flashed back.

She waited a moment to see if this startling bulletin might impress the folks in front of her, but they were all too busy *shmoozing* and no one stoppped. Aunt Sophia inclined her head toward me, "Desperate situations require desperate measures," she muttered. I didn't have long to wonder what she meant by that.

Moving closer to the man in front of her, she leaned harder against her cane, exaggerating her appearance of disability. Poking him to be sure she had his undivided attention, she confided earnestly, and in a *very* loud voice, "I've had a *very serious* accident, and I can't stand on my feet too long." She gazed at him with a pitiful expression, neglecting to mention that the accident had occurred five years before.

The man blanched and began to fidget. A minute ticked by, then another. Aunt Sophia continued to hold him in her thrall. The poor guy looked as if he'd rather be on some other planet, but he *didn't* offer to trade his place with her.

Aunt Sophia cranked the pathos up a notch. "These are my beloved niece and nephew who came *all* the way from *Canada* just to visit me."

The man acknowledged us with a nervous nod. "They're *very* hungry," she added, implying we hadn't eaten for days.

Stanley and I grinned at each other. God help the poor fellow. She'd never release him now!

Gazing even more deeply into the eyes of her hero, Aunt Sophia allowed a flicker of brave hope to illumine her trusting face. He coughed and darted a look at the harried hostess. A sheen of fine sweat dampened *his* twitching face.

From Aunt Sophia's point of view, things were progressing nicely. It was now time to deliver the *coup-de-grace!*

"Oooy!" she groaned, affecting a little stagger. **"I'm in so much pain!** I'm not even supposed to be on my feet!" There was a murmuring and shuffling among the proletariat.

"Why don't you sit over there while you wait?" suggested a well-meaning lady. She pointed to an empty bench beside the wall. But Aunt Sophia didn't want to wait on benches. She wanted to be taken out of turn and seated now!

Turning a deaf ear to the advice of the interloper, Aunt Sophia signaled the receptionist.

"Tell me, honey. Is Monica here today?"

The distracted receptionist said "Yes."

"Ask her to come here, honey. I have something to tell her." The receptionist looked doubtful, but obeyed. She plunged into the maelstrom of crowded tables, noisy diners, and harassed waitresses in search of Monica. In about five minutes she returned. "Monica will be right out."

Aunt Sophia, finding herself at an impasse, rekindled her relationship with the man in front of her. He listened without speaking, just moving his lips, as if he'd begun to pray.

Soon a gaunt looking waitress appeared. "I'm Monica," she said.

Aunt Sophia looked skeptical." I meant the *fat* Monica. Is the *fat* Monica in today?"

Gaunt Monica said she was the *only* Monica in the restaurant.

"Oh. All right honey, listen. I've had a very bad accident and I'm not supposed to be on my feet. Here are my beloved niece and nephew who came all the way from Canada to visit me. They're *very* hungry. Do you think you could find a table for us right away?"

Aunt Sophia smiled wanly at Monica. Monica gazed helplessly into Aunt Sophia's innocent face. "I'll see what I can do," she mumbled, and melted into the mayhem.

Aunt Sophia, still brimming with the milk of human kindness, turned back to the poor fish who still wriggled on the end of her line. His hat was awry, his shirt front had wilted, he looked shredded, somehow—as if he had just walked through an electric fan.

All this time we had been inching slowly forward. Step by step toward our hostess, until now it was his turn. Aunt Sophia cut him loose with a wave of regret. It was always hard to let the big ones go.

Wondering what had become of Monica, I glanced at Aunt Sophia's face. Was she angry? Disappointed? None of her ploys had worked. She shrugged. "You never know till you try ..." she said, and winked. When the receptionist returned, Aunt Sophia limped cheerfully after her to our table.

Wouldn't you know it? Monica turned out to be our waitress. With lowered eyes, she apologized for not being able to get back. Aunt Sophia accepted her apology gracefully. "It's O.K. honey, at least you tried."

Monica presented the menus.

"What's good, honey? Is it fresh?"

How many times had I witnessed this catechism? Magical lunches by Johnson's, strawberry shortcake at Virginia Dare. I could taste the steak I always ordered at Miller Brothers. She'd turn to me. "How do you want it honey?"

I'd say "Medium."

She'd turn to Metz, our waiter. "She'll have well done. Don't let it be too rare!"

I couldn't remember a time when Aunt Sophia wasn't feeding me. Not only with delicious food, but with warmth and love, and laughter. I smiled across the table at my husband. How nice, I thought. We're getting to feed her for a change.

Now that we were seated, Aunt Sophia was in no rush to order. Not only did she take great care selecting her own dishes, she also felt obliged to pass judgment on ours. Poor Monica was looking more haggard by the minute. Her eyes darted around the room. Desperation clung to her pinched face.

Finally, after grilling Monica for seven and a half minutes on each side, Aunt Sophia gave her our orders and allowed her to return to the kitchen. Once, in a similar situation, my mother had attempted to restrain her irrepressible sister. "Soph," she'd muttered out of the corner of her mouth, "you're keeping the woman waiting."

Aunt Sophia's eyes had widened with the innocence of childhood. "Well, she's a *waitress* isn't she?"

Her labors completed, Aunt Sophia sat back with a satisfied sigh and surveyed her domain. "This is my niece and nephew who came all the way from Canada to visit me," she began, hailing the man sitting alone at the next table. Before long they were kibitzing like old buddies. She even worked him into our table conversation. Soon the lady at the table next to him was included, then the couple next to her. Aunt Sophia was a born social director. All she needed was a room full of people. Then, like Penelope, she could weave her spell.

I marveled at the way she kept the interest going—twining our separate threads in and around each other till we became a lively and colorful whole. Everyone on our side of the room was hysterical. They laughed and joked, and seemed to be having a wonderful time. I looked at Aunt Sophia. Her eyes sparkled with merriment, and her generous body jiggled with laughter. She was having the best time of all.

She regaled us with stories of her telephone exploits on a late night radio show.

"When I called in to give them my opinion, they asked me my name. So I told them Jessica."

"Jessica?" I repeated. "Why?"

"So then somebody else calls in and says, 'I agree with Jessica!'"

Aunt Sophia and the geriatric set howled. I still didn't get it so I just smiled.

"Did you know that the most beautiful woman in the world is deaf?" she asked with a perfectly straight face.

"No. I didn't know that, Aunt Sophia."

"WHAT?" she yelled, cupping her hand around her ear and cocking her head. This time even I collapsed.

All too soon the meal was over. We bundled her back into the car, and drove to her apartment. She was still fizzing with good spirits. We helped her up the stairway, and waited while she unlocked the door. "You want anything honey? How about some grapes?"

"No thank you, Aunt Sophia, I'm full."

"How about you Stanley. Have some grapes!"

"No, thank you Aunt Sophia."

"I wish we could stay and visit, but we really have to go."

"I know, honey. I wish you could too."

I hugged her hard.

"Thanks for coming to visit me, hear? It was wonderful to see you. Are the girls all right? Give them both a kiss from their old Aunt Sophia. And that shmoogle-poogle Maxi too."

She kissed Stanley. "Thanks for taking me out to lunch Stanley, I had a wonderful time. I hope it didn't cost you too much."

"It was my pleasure, Aunt Sophia. I enjoyed it too."

"Have a safe trip back, now, hear? Write when you get home, you owe me a letter."

"You mean a visit doesn't count, Aunt Sophia?"

"A visit is a visit—not a letter! It's your turn to write to me."

"O.K. Aunt Sophia, I'll write."

"You sure you don't want any grapes? You can take them in the car. No? O.K. Good-bye honey. I'll wave from the window. Have a safe trip back, now, hear?"

For one precious afternoon, she had been my old Aunt Sophia. It was terrible to have to let her go.

We pulled out of the driveway waving. She smiled, waving back, and blew a kiss. Aunt Sophia had been blowing me kisses for fifty years. Even on the telephone. "Here it comes, honey, SMACK! Did you get it?"

"I got it. Here comes one for you. SMACK!"

Two months later we were back for her funeral. She had died suddenly from pneumonia, like Joe. By the time anyone heard she was sick it had been too late.

Why? How? Aunt Sophia's been here forever! How could she just die like that?

I listened to the Rabbi drone through the service. I was numb, asleep—yet I *ached* with grief. Stanley stood beside me, his hand on my shoulder.

I looked across at Gischa. Her face was closed, completely blank. *I guess it hasn't hit her yet.*

My gaze shifted to the closed coffin. Where are you Aunt Sophia? *I know you're not in there!*

"She must have been ready," I whispered to Stanley. "Aunt Sophia never did a thing in her life until she was ready. Being alone was too hard for her. She must have decided it was time to go."

At the cemetery, I watched some men unload her casket. *They'll carry it to the plot and bury it. I'll never see her again!*

"Wait! Please, I have to say good-bye." Stanley was right beside me, supporting me as always. The men hesitated, looking sour. Uncle Harry stepped forward. "Open it. Now!"

Oh God, will I recognize her? I've never seen a dead person!

With sullen faces, the men lifted the cover. There lay Aunt Sophia, beautiful as always. *Why, she only looks asleep!* I traced the curve of her beloved cheek with my index finger. *She looks so quiet, so peaceful.*

Then I stroked the place on her forehead where she'd had the deepest crease. It felt smooth and cool and waxy. "I love you, Aunt Sophia," I whispered and blew her a kiss. The men came and closed the casket. We mumbled some prayers, and I watched them lower her into the ground.

The family gathered at my cousin Sandy's. People came to pay their respects. I tried to, but I couldn't *hear* what they were saying. All I heard was the echo in my own head—*Aunt Sophia, please! Don't go, don't go...*

Six p.m. We all went out for dinner. My uncle said he knew of a place nearby. In the station wagon, conversation swirled around me. A single phrase pounded inside my skull: *don't go, don't go, don't go!*

Larry parked and we trailed along behind him—across the asphalt to a line of stores.

"This is it," Uncle Harry said.

I looked up, and my heart *grizhid* within me.

"Manny's," blinked the sign over the door.

Wear it Well

"Did you wash your hands?" Gischa demanded as she and I exited the ladies room. I nodded, taking note of the mischievous gleam in her eye.

"Did you?" I countered. We both laughed.

Gischa said, "Whenever I use a public restroom, I still hear Aunt Sophia urging, 'Wash your hands honey,' like she did when I was little. I don't think I could *not* wash my hands now, even if I wanted to!"

Maybe that's what immortality is all about, I mused—someone living on inside you, continuing to instruct, cajole and influence—whether you want them to or not. If my theory is true, then Aunt Sophia has certainly achieved immortality in our family. She shpritzed us so often, and so lavishly, with her verbal benedictions, they filtered through our skin, bored deep into our psyches, and became fixed—impervious to time, maturity, or the ravages of modern life.

Words were Aunt Sophia's stock in trade; her currency for securing our safe passage in an unpredictable and dangerous world. She repeated certain phrases so often and with such insistence they became incantations. One of her favorites was "wear it well." Whenever I got something new, Aunt Sophia always noticed. "Is that a new dress honey? It's beautiful! Wear it well. *A gizent in dir!*"

I had heard that phrase a zillion times growing up, but not once since I lost Aunt Sophia. Imagine my surprise the day I reached for my raincoat—a raincoat I had been wearing all along—and noticed a flash of white. I peered closer.

Someone had stitched a narrow rectangular label into the collar. *Wear in Good Health,* I read.

Those delicate wisps of hair on the back of my neck sprang to attention. Aunt Sophia! I could hear the familiar cadence of her loving and beloved voice. Had I really believed that anything could still Aunt Sophia?

How does she *do* these things? I wondered. Has that tag always been there? If it has, then why have I never noticed it? Is mine the only coat that carries this injunction? If it is, then how did *I* come to choose this one?

As usual, where Aunt Sophia was concerned, I had plenty of questions but a conspicuous lack of answers. In a universe filled with mysteries she remains, for me, one of the biggest and most mysterious.

I reread the legend, welcoming the warm rush of comfort her memory always inspires. Pulling the garment close about me, I felt embraced by the soft protecting pressure of Aunt Sophia's *zoftig* arms.

I haven't really lost her, I thought. I couldn't—she's part of me. She is in my mind, and heart—ye gods, she's even in my raincoat! No pale ephemeral wraithe-like spirit she, but solid and robust as always. She pops in often and unexpectedly, still keeping a watchful eye on a much-loved niece. I shouldn't be surprised. No one in our family has ever been good at saying good-bye.

"Say *ken ahora!*" she entreats when I rave about my grandchildren.

"Have some, honey, it's *good* for you," she pleads when I consider eating something fattening.

I think of her a hundred times a day and hug her to me whenever I feel frightened or lose my courage. She warms me with all the force of life she once carried within her—and still does as far as I can tell. What a gift she has given me!

Living in Southern California I don't often get to wear a raincoat, so each time I see Aunt Sophia's blessing, I am startled anew.

Wear in Good Health. Thank you Aunt Sophia. With your help, I'm wearing as well as I can.

"How ya Doin', Doc?"

Irvin

Now, finally, it's Uncle Irvin's turn to bask in the glow of the spotlight. He has waited patiently, as usual, for Aunt Sophia to relinquish center stage. Even death doesn't change some things. Thirty-six years is a long time to stand in the wings, but Uncle Irvin never seemed to mind. Had he been nominated for an Oscar, it would have been for Best Supporting Player. I can't think of anyone who deserved it more.

When he proposed to Aunt Sophia, he knew she'd never leave her mother. He also understood that her family came first—period—and always would. Not only did he accept those conditions graciously, he embraced them with his whole heart. Like Ruth in the Bible, her people became his. He married all of us when he married Aunt Sophia, and happily spent the rest of his life showering us with devotion, loyalty, and unconditional love. Especially the children, on whom he kept—without hovering—a close and benevolent eye.

I remember the summer I was eight, when all the kids in the neighborhood were collecting matchbooks. We'd scrounge them from the gutter and catalogue them in shoeboxes. The idea was to get as many different brands as possible so you could trade them, like baseball cards. I loved collecting things, and I especially loved exploring gutters.

Irvin

Some of the specimens I found were pretty grungy. When Mother discovered my "collection," she nearly *plotzed*.

"Jo-*Ann*. They're full of *germs!*"

"Soooo? Everybody's doing it. I need to get as many as I can so I'll have the biggest collection. There's lots of good ones just lying in the street—and they're free!"

As economical as Mother usually was, my logic did not impress her. She pulled herself up to her full five feet two inches, took a deep breath, and announced: "Jo-Ann, I forbid you to collect any more matchbooks from any more gutters, and if I find out you disobeyed me I'll...I'll...*punish* you *severely!*"

"Oh please, please! I won't get sick, I promise."

"The subject, is closed!" She stamped on the pedal of the metal container, the round lid flipped up, and she dumped my carefully scavenged treasure into the garbage. "Now, go and wash your hands!"

Of course The Family heard all about it, and as soon as they heard the word "germs," they were one hundred per cent behind her. The next time they came over, Bubby padded up to me in her hesitant way.

"It no be's good, Jo-Vennala. Siz shmutzik!" she quavered, gazing into my eyes with her large solemn brown ones.

She clapped her palm against her face and shook her head sadly, as if she could already picture the terrible calamity about to befall me.

Aunt Sophia took up the cry. "What do you need them for honey? They're dirty. Feh! Don't do it, it's not good!" She paused. "Tell her Irv."

Uncle Irvin turned his big blue eyes on me. He looked sad. "Listen to Aunt Sophia, honey," he urged kindly, "she's right."

I was crushed. *Nobody* understood. Not even my fairy godparents! Now I'd never have the most matchbooks. I wouldn't have any matchbooks at all!

At lunch time the next day, Uncle Irvin rang our front door bell. I peered at him through the screen. His face looked serious, and his arms were bulging with cardboard boxes that were stacked up right to his chin.

"Here, honey," he extended them toward me, "these are for you."

I stared at the flat white boxes. It wasn't my birthday—and they weren't wrapped in fancy paper—what could be in them? There wasn't even any writing on the side to give me a clue. I opened the first box and stared, dumbfounded at the contents. Lined up like soldiers standing at attention, was row upon row of crisp new match books. Hundreds of them! I'd never seen so many in one place in my life.

"How...?" I began. "Where...?"

"Enjoy them in good health, honey," he said. He turned to leave.

"Let Mother tear out all the matches before you play with them, hear?" And he was gone. With one loving gesture he had transformed me, a neighborhood nobody, into The Queen of Collectors. I couldn't believe my good luck.

And I wasn't the only one who received such loving attention. When Larry was little, Uncle Irvin spent hours squatting beside him on the edge of the rug in our living room. Larry watched as Uncle Irvin, tense with excitement, sent the cars and trucks he had brought skimming wildly across the shiny wooden floor. "Varoom! Screech! Boom!" roared Uncle Irvin. His eyes gleamed maniacally behind the swishing fringe of dark hair that had collapsed onto his forehead.

"I wonder who's having the most fun?" Mother observed, as she made her way past them to the kitchen. On her face was the merest suggestion of a smile.

By the time Larry was three, Uncle Irvin was coaching him to perfect his pitch. Larry would wind up, twist his body to the right, raise his left leg, lower it, kick his right leg back, and let the ball rip.

"Just like Bobby Feller!" Uncle Irvin would yell. "Atta boy, Lar! Soph! Look at that arm! The kid's gonna be a professional!"

He never seemed to tire of our company. Instead, he found us endlessly absorbing. He was the only adult who listened—really listened—to our feelings, not just our words.

When I was thirteen, I was allowed, after much discussion, to take the train to New York to visit a cousin. By myself. Although the trip had been my idea, and I had pushed very hard for permission, I was nervous about the train station. I had seen some scary looking characters hanging around down there. Mother and Daddy would see me off, but when I came back it would be the middle of a workday. Mother didn't drive, and Daddy would be out on his debit. I would have to take the streetcar.

Going home on the streetcar didn't bother me. I'd been "riding the rails" alone since I was six. It was getting safely out of the station. I was small for my age, and my recently acquired bosom made me feel vulnerable. I had overheard the grownups discussing newspaper stories about young girls being raped. Suppose one of those characters came after me? The more I thought about it, the more terrified I felt.

On the Sunday evening before I left, The Family was visiting, as usual. Of course the main topic of conversation was my trip. Bubby kept watching me, as waves of pleasure, amazement and anxiety chased each other across her lined face. She appeared to have me confused with Amelia Earhart; as if I were attempting a solo flight around the world. Perhaps she was remembering her own young womanhood, and the courage she'd needed to travel to America alone.

Aunt Sophia vacillated between worry and admiration. "Will you be all right, honey? Do you know where to go?" Then she'd turn to Uncle Irvin, "Can you imagine that monkey? Off to New York all by herself." To me she said, "You're something, girl, you're really something!"

"I want Uncle Irvin to pick me up in his cab," I blurted suddenly.

Aunt Sophia looked surprised. "Why, honey?" Mother and Daddy also asked why. But I was too ashamed to tell them. I was brave enough to go all the way to New York by myself, but I was afraid to be alone in the Baltimore train station. "I just do, that's all. I want Uncle Irvin to pick me up in the cab."

Mother, Daddy, and Aunt Sophia fired questions at me. What's all the tumult about? I wondered. Uncle Irvin drives a cab. He picks up people at the station all the time. I'm his niece, why shouldn't he pick me up too?

Uncle Irvin listened until there was a break in the conversation. Then he asked, his voice oh so gentle, "You want me to pick you up, honey?" His eyes seemed to look straight into my soul.

I nodded, too choked up to risk talking.

"What time does your train get in?"

"Two o' clock," I murmured.

"I'll be there, honey. Don't you worry 'bout a thing."

A week later, when I got off the train he was there, waiting for me on the platform. His face lit up when he saw me. With one burly arm he swept me close against him. With the other he took my suitcase. I burrowed into his thick chest the way I'd burrow into an oversized quilt during a thunderstorm. He felt so warm and strong and comforting!

Escorting me past the grubby layabouts with the dignity he would have bestowed on a real lady, he handed me into the waiting cab, and chauffered me safely home. It wasn't until years later that I realized: he could have been earning his living that afternoon. He had chosen instead to rescue me.

When Gischa started dating, Uncle Irvin appointed himself her chief guardian angel. He made sure that he and Aunt Sophia arrived at our house at least one-half hour before the boy did. While Aunt Sophia kibbitzed inside with the family, Uncle Irvin stationed himself on the porch for a casual smoke. From this vantage point, he could observe not only the make and model of the car the poor guy was driving, he could assess the young man's driving ability as well.

Uncle Irvin's two hundred and fifty pound body would be the first thing the boy encountered as he approached our house. Such an apparition looming suddenly out of the darkness must have given an already nervous young man pause.

Uncle Irvin's face would widen into a welcoming grin as he pumped the boy's hand with vigor.

"Jaslow's the name, (pump pump) how're you do'in, Doc? I'm Gischa's Uncle Irvin."

Having put the date at ease, Uncle Irvin would then escort the unsuspecting creature inside and introduce him to the rest of the family. As he stepped over the threshold, eight curious pairs of eyes bored into him with the insistence of a Black and Decker drill. There would have been nine, but Gischa was still upstairs. She was ready, but she didn't want her date to think she was over-anxious. Aunt Sophia presided in Gischa's absence. Uncle Irvin waited patiently for his cue.

"Hi, honey, what's your name?" she'd ask, as if she hadn't just heard it. "Applebaum? Are you related to Sol Applebaum from Cold Spring Lane?"

If the boy said no, she'd produce a few more Applebaums for his consideration.

"How about Manny Applebaum, the one with the drug store up on Park Heights Avenue?"

If she couldn't find a connection, Uncle Irvin stepped in. He would then recall every Applebaum he'd ever known or read about, until Gischa's date claimed a relative, no matter how far distant. When they had exhausted that topic, Aunt Sophia pressed on.

"So where do you live, honey?"

"On Barrington Road."

"Oh. Barrington Road. That's a nice neighborhood." Then she'd turn to Uncle Irvin. "Barrington Road, Irv."

Uncle Irvin smoothed back his hair. "Barrington Road, huh? I just picked up a guy on Barrington Road the other day. Forty-one hundred block. Fella by the name of Epstein. You know him?"

The boy shook his head.

"Has a furniture store down on Monument street."

"I live in the forty hundred block Barrington."

"Oh."

Back to Aunt Sophia. "So, what do you do, Sheldon? Have you been driving long? What kind of business is your father in?"

Each answer led to another question. Periodically, Uncle Irvin would intervene to enlarge on some point which he found interesting. He always encouraged the boy to share his own views as well. When Aunt Sophia got to the end of her catechism, she'd begin again.

"Did you have to drive far to get here?"

Aunt Sophia and Uncle Irvin did not bother with the big questions like, "Where are you going?" or "What time will you be back?" Those were Mother and Daddy's prerogative. They preferred to concentrate on the smaller issues: the boy's family, his politics, his economic expectations, his hopes, his dreams, and his aspirations.

Gischa's date, who had sunk into a kind of stupor during the inquisition, revived when he saw my sister sashay down the stairs. She was all "*fah-pittzed*," as Daddy would say, and really did look beautiful. Everyone ooohhhed and aahhhhed. The boy blushed as he helped Gischa on with her coat. Uncle Irvin sauntered over and kissed her good-night. Then he accompanied them both to the front door and watched as they started down the walk to the car.

"Y'all have a nice time, and drive careful now, hear?"

The rest of us ogled from the living room window.

"My niece sure did look purtty tonight, didn't she?" Uncle Irvin mused as they vroomed off into the darkness. "Did you-all see how he blushed when she came downstairs?" Uncle Irvin took out a cigarette, tamped it down on the end of his lighter, and clamped it between his lips. Stretching his beefy arms out in front of him, he engaged the fingers of his right hand against the fingers of his left and pulled. Crraacck! His knuckles went off like a pistol shot.

"'Course, that young man better behave himself around my niece," drawled Uncle Irvin out of the small opening left between the clamped cigarette, and the corner of his mouth, "otherwise her Ole Uncle Irvin might have to drive on over to the forty hundred block of Barrington Road and give him a lesson or two on how a gentleman treats a lady."

Good! I thought. It was comforting to know that when it came my turn to date, I'd have a two hundred and fifty (give or take a few) pound guardian angel looking over my shoulder.

Partners

When Uncle Irvin married Aunt Sophia, he understood that he would never play more than second violin in the Shapiro Family Orchestra. Aunt Sophia was, and always would be both Concert Mistress and Conductor. But he had been smitten, and had rushed to sign a life-time contract. Throughout their thirty-six years together, he was happy to play pianissimo accompaniment to her fortissimo melody. Most of the time, the music they made together was sweet and harmonius. There were, however, occasional dissonances.

Although the rest of us regarded Uncle Irvin as a paragon of patience, Aunt Sophia often complained. "*You* know," she'd say to me, "you know your old Uncle Irvin. I say *one thing* and right away he gets crazy. *He hollers!*" She always seemed bemused by this behavior, convinced that it could have nothing to do with her. "What did I say?" she'd demand, "I only told the truth!"

When he did lose his temper, he'd blow up quickly, like a summer storm. His face reddened, his body swelled, and his eyes darkened and shot forth sparks of lightning. He'd bellow for about two minutes, causing his cream-oiled pompador to collapse over his forehead in a fringe of inverted commas. Then he'd smile sheepishly, smooth back his hair, and blot his perspiring forehead with a gigantic white handkerchief. His eyes lightened from midnight back to baby blue, and his whole being became peaceful.

We were only amazed he didn't explode more often. Much as we loved her, we knew Aunt Sophia could drive a saint to drink. Even Bubby allowed herself one small criticism of her loyally steadfast daughter. She declared Aunt Sophia perfect except for the *one tiny* vein she'd inherited from Zady. I think Mother said it best when she recalled her own exasperating years under the same roof with her older sister, "It's very hard to live with Aunt Sophia and not holler."

I thought Uncle Irvin deserved a medal for living with Aunt Sophia all those years without losing his romantic illusions. Not to mention his sanity. Whenever Aunt Sophia was perplexed about something, she would first *dray* her own *kup* for a while. "What should I do?" she would murmur rhetorically. "I don't know what to do." Then she'd turn to Uncle Irvin. "What do *you* think, Irv?"

Uncle Irvin prided himself on being well-read, and loved to expound on a variety of topics. He would smile broadly, puff up his chest, straighten his shoulders and declaim for some time. Throughout his monologue she would gaze at him enraptured, as though he were Moses delivering the law from Mount Sinai.

When he finally wound down, she would fix him with a disdainful eye, dismiss him with a wave of her hand and say, "Aw, what do *you* know, you drive a cab." Then, in case whoever else in the room hadn't heard, she would turn down the corners of her mouth, shake her head from side to side, and repeat in a louder voice, "*He* doesn't know; he drives a cab!"

If his feelings were hurt, he never showed it. I'd search his face for signs that he was wounded, but there were none. His demeanor remained placid and forebearing, his blue eyes stayed innocent as a child's.

I don't think Uncle Irvin realized he was marrying a confirmed secrets addict. Aunt Sophia and Bubby kept secrets from Zady, from the rest of the family, and from the

U.S. government. They even kept secrets from each other. When Uncle Irvin joined The Family, they added him to the already long list of people who were not in the know.

One of the biggest secrets was Aunt Sophia's age. She refused to let anyone in on the *emes*—especially Uncle Irvin. Those who knew she swore to secrecy. She even falsified official documents. Every paper she signed had a different birthdate on it, including her marriage license. Aunt Sophia was thirty-five years old when she married Uncle Irvin. He was twenty-two. The license lists them both as twenty-eight. Uncle Irvin knew she was older; he just didn't know by how much. Aunt Sophia was determined to keep *that* a state secret. She spent the next thirty years frantically manipulating the family statistics. Each time she dropped a few years from herself, she had to make Bubby and Zady younger too.

There were times when Aunt Sophia had to do some pretty fancy juggling to keep her charade aloft, but she was more than equal to it. When Uncle Irvin made noises about having children, she said she had a bad back, and pregnancy wasn't good for her. Did she think she was too old? Was she afraid of the responsibility? Was she afraid a child might separate her from Uncle Irvin the way she had separated Bubby from Zady? Who knows? Whatever the reason, she insisted it was because of her back. Uncle Irvin deferred to her as he always did, though he yearned for children of his own.

"Have this one for me, Mary," he said to my mother when he heard another baby was on the way. "Can I be the godfather?" He was ecstatic when my parents said yes. When Larry was born Uncle Irvin was jubilant. *Baruch Hashem!* He finally had his boy! Aunt Sophia had denied him his dream, but he loved her so much, he could transcend even that.

When she went through menopause and was behaving irrationally, she claimed it was his mother's fault. She couldn't admit that she was old enough to "go through the change." She wouldn't even tell her own doctor the truth. She reported to Uncle Irvin: "The doctor said 'stay away from your in-laws, they make you nervous.'"

This too he accepted, although I'm sure it hurt him. Then she insisted that he avoid them too. He loved his wife, even though she demanded one hundred percent of his time, love, and loyalty. But, he also loved his family. He took the only course she had left him. He went to see his mother and brothers and sisters on the sly.

Who could even begin to understand such a marriage? It was so complex, so riddled with contradictions. I wonder if even *they* understood it. Perhaps they were too busy living it to try. They needed each other, and that need bound them together as if they were interlocking pieces of wet cement. By the time the cement dried, their original boundaries had disappeared forever.

We called them AuntSophiandUncleIrvin, as if together they shared one name. They were partners, in every sense of the word. If they came over to see us and I was crabby or impolite, Aunt Sophia would say, "She's tired," or "She's hungry, Irv."

"We'll be right out of your way honey," Uncle Irvin would say, without a trace of anger or hurt feelings. He understood.

In an era when children were expected to be "seen and not heard," they not only listened to our thoughts and feelings, they treated us with dignity and respect. They lavished us with love, expensive presents, and attention, then raved over any small gesture we might make in return.

"Soph! Look at the beautiful card that monkey made for us."

"Oh, honey, thank you, thank you. It's beautiful! *Ken Ahora.*"

Their faces shone with such pleasure and gratitude, as if I had given them a rare jewel instead of a home-made valentine scrawled in my primitive hand.

They were both careful about hurting people's feelings, especially loved ones. If they praised one of us, they praised us all. Years later when we were grown and married they included our spouses in the same way.

"And let's not forget about Stanley!" Uncle Irvin would say, if Aunt Sophia waxed too poetic over me. She would immediately pick up her cue and find a reason to compliment Stanley.

They each had a passion for good food and loved eating out. They generously shared their zeal with anyone they could get to listen.

"You should try this new Greek restaurant we ate at, Mary." Uncle Irvin's face was flushed, and his eyes sparkled with excitement.

"The food is really delicious," Aunt Sophia jumped in.

"We tried this wine called Mavrodavne. They put a slice of apple in it when they serve it. You and Kit have to try it. It's terrific!"

They loved to shmooze, and struck up conversations with total strangers wherever they went. People were attracted by their open-heartedness and child-like enthusiasm. Their enjoyment of each other was so great, it spilled on to anyone who was lucky enough to be with them. Even politics, one of their favorite topics of conversation, besides us, they argued good-naturedly.

Uncle Irvin was so much on Aunt Sophia's wave length, he understood her even when she got *tsemished*. Like the time Aunt Sophia and Bubby took a ride with us "in the machine." For some reason, Uncle Irvin couldn't go and Daddy ended up driving. Aunt Sophia announced she'd like to go out to Loch Raven, which was a considerable distance away. Daddy dutifully drove us there. All during the trip, Aunt Sophia rhapsodized about the beauties of Loch Raven.

Partners

When we finally got there, she looked dismayed." *This* isn't Loch Raven!" she insisted.

Daddy's voice got a little testy. "Yes it is, Soph, look at the sign!"

"Ohhh," murmured Aunt Sophia. "I *said* Loch Raven, but I *meant* Montebello." There was a short pause, then she added with authority, " *Irvin* would have known!"

After twenty-five years of marriage, Uncle Irvin still grew lyrical about his Lady.

"Aunt Sophia gets so pretty in the summer!" he confided to me one day. His own face softened as he described the creamy luster of her sun-kissed skin, the sensuous curves of her golden body, and the shimmer of her sun-lightened hair.

Pain and sorrow were not allowed to mar the joy they took in each other's company. Throughout their long and happy marriage, they remained companions, lovers—friends. Aunt Sophia and Uncle Irvin knew each other's frailities well, but they decided to love each other anyway. Together they created a relationship which nurtured and sustained them both for thirty-six years. Till death did them part.

Teamwork

Uncle Irvin loved all his nieces and nephews, but somehow he made me feel special. All I had to do was look in his eyes, and I could see the love. It was a very heady feeling for a little girl. I knew—from the tender age of two—that he was my biggest fan.

"Soph! Soph! Listen to this!" he would holler, then repeat my latest observation as though he were quoting Einstein. Whatever I did was remarkable. He never seemed to grow tired of my company or of accosting unsuspecting friends, waitresses, or fares in his cab with, "Let me tell you about my niece Jo-Ann. That monkey. She's big as a minute, but smart as a whip. You won't believe what that little *bandit* did *this* time!"

He made me feel beautiful; as beautiful and sought after as Scarlet O'Hara. And he was my broad-shouldered, mushtachioed handsome young Rhett. In a moment of quiet confidence, I told him my secret.

"You know what, Uncle Irvin? You look just like Clark Gable in the movies." I watched his forty-five inch chest expand about eight more inches.

"Soph! Soph! Wait till you hear this! Tell Aunt Sophia what you just said, honey." But before I could speak he blurted, "She thinks I look like Clark Gable! Can you beat that?"

I had clearly, and quite innocently, made his day.

Not only was Uncle Irvin handsome, he was also brave and dashing. Maybe he didn't leap over balconies fencing furiously, like Douglas Fairbanks or Erroll Flynn, but he laughed in the face of danger just like they did. Hadn't he come back from overseas not only unhurt, but unruffled? Compared to the rest of the family—who acted as if we were always on the edge of an abyss, and only just around the corner from catastrophe—Uncle Irvin was calm and reassuring. When I was with him, I knew no harm could ever come to me.

I remember a trick we performed together, although I must have been less than two at the time. Picture a miniature Mahatma Ghandi: a tiny skinny body, hardly any hair, and skin kind of yellowy brown. For this trick to work we needed our muscles, our courage, and all of our self-discipline.

"Come on over here, honey," Uncle Irvin would say, bending his knees and laying his right hand down in the street, palm upward. Then, lifting me with his left arm, he'd stand me in the middle of his outstretched palm and support me till I got my balance. As soon as I was secure, he'd nod. That was my cue to stand straight as a little soldier, while he stiffened his hand and arm till they were rigid as a tabletop.

We looked deep in each other's eyes. Then Uncle Irvin removed his supporting hand and I felt the thrill of delicious danger! If I lost my concentration for a second, or moved even a smigeon, I would fall.

Uncle Irvin talked to me. His words were soft and encouraging as he slowly straightened his bent knees and raised his upturned palm with me on it—up, up, up like an elevator, till I was high in the air!

"Atta girl, Jo, you can do it. Don't move now. You can do it." His eyes bulged, and sweat poured off him like shower water. His arm shook with strain, but he kept his hand flat and solid. I stood motionless, legs stiff, arms tight against my sides, overcoming by sheer will my usual inclination to wiggle. Maintaining that level of control wasn't easy, but it was worth it for the look of pride I saw shining on Uncle Irvin's purple face.

I was pretty proud of myself, come to think about it. It felt good to feel so tall and brave and free. One twitch—his or mine—could send me flying, but *my* Uncle Irvin would *never* let me hit the ground.

"Hold on honey, goin' down." As soon as I touched *terra firma* he grabbed me with a beefy arm. "Good for you, Doc," he whispered, smashing me hard against his chest. When he straightened his legs, I came only as high as his knees, but I felt as if I were ten feet tall.

A few years later, when I grew too big to fit in his hand, he invented a new trick. This time he stretched his arm straight out in front of him, and I stood facing him underneath.

"O. K., Jo." Reaching over my head with both hands I glommed on to his mighty forearm while he closed his paw into a huge fist. We stared at each other. I made my body stiff as cardboard. Uncle Irvin grit his teeth. His arm shook and quaked like Jello, but up I came, my legs dangling in the air.

Higher and higher he struggled to raise me, egging me on with his eyes that were starting farther and farther out of his head. I could feel his veins twitch, and his muscles ripple; then I felt the sweat come, and my fingers start to slip.

Uncle Irvin's face had frozen into a fright mask. Like a slow motion movie running backwards, he brought me down millimeter by millimeter till I was on my feet. He mopped his face with his handkerchief, "You did great, Doc." I could see he was pleased. Was it because he could raise me with one arm, or because I believed in him with such absolute trust?

If Aunt Sophia caught us practicing she would get all *coxcited*. "Irv, Irv, put her down, you'll hurt her!" But Uncle Irvin would just wink at me and say, "She's fine Soph, she's just fine." And with him—of course—I really was!

Eh-Heh-Heh-Heh-Chhemm!

Although Uncle Irvin was "only an in-law," he was built like everyone else on my mother's side of the family—close to the ground and *square*. At 5' 8" he was an inch shorter than my father, but a lot heavier. His stocky body, which fluctuated between 250 and 275 pounds, sported a thick layer of fat, over an even thicker layer of well-developed muscle.

"Watch this, honey," he'd coax as he slid back his shirt sleeve, crooked his arm and exposed his bulging bicep.

My eyes widened with wonder and admiration.

"Feel how hard it is!"

Gingerly, I'd extend my index finger and poke it as it bounced and undulated beneath the skin.

"Ohhhh!" I'd squeal, "it's like a rock!"

That was just what he'd been waiting for. He'd smile with his whole face and puff out his chest like a bellows. The regular meeting of our mutual admiration society had begun!

Uncle Irvin was my hedge against terrifying nightmares. His sturdy legs hugged the ground like the roots of a mighty oak tree. His trunk widened into a vast barrel chest capped by powerful brawny shoulders and beefy arms. I sought shelter under his leafy branches. Nyah, nyah, no scary demons could get me here!

He was my touchstone with reality; the only grown-up I knew who wasn't scared to death. The only time I saw him even falter was the summer night my mother cleared her throat.

My mother had turned the simple act of clearing her throat into an art form; a kind of Conalrad alert that told us trouble was on the way. We learned early to distinguish an actual throat-clearing, which sounded benign and superficial, from the dangerous one—which sounded like the knell of doom.

First came the warning "eh-heh-heh," from deep in her throat which instantly caught our attention. Then she'd turn up the volume, speed up the momentum, and crescendo into an explosive "chhemm!" which always took the top of my head off, and never failed to stand my hair on end. An ominous silence followed as we pondered the coming catastrophe. Mother reserved this tactic for special occasions, when she wanted us to know that she was *furious* but—for the moment at least—under control.

The entire neighborhood was familiar with my mother's repertoire. These vocal missives had punctuated the tempo of our daily lives for years. Our frequent misbehaviors and the "well-meant" interference of her Family often pushed her to the brink. Sometimes she'd prowl the house muttering through clenched teeth, "I'm gonna commit murder. So help me, I'm gonna commit *murder!*" That was always my cue to beat a hasty retreat.

A large part of the conflict between Mother and her Family involved disagreements about how to raise us. Mother believed in: enforcing rules, schedules, and early curfews, limiting sweets, and encouraging self-discipline and hard work. Both she and my father regarded doing without as the only sure way to "build character."

Enter Aunt Sophia and Uncle Irvin and the fairy godparents theory of child-rearing. "A child is a child and has a right to expect happiness!" So, they interrupted our naps, kept us up past our bedtime, fed us sweets, indulged our whims, showered us with presents, and "spoiled us rotten."

"Schedules?" questioned Aunt Sophia? "What is this—the army? Who needs schedules? Feh!"

In an effort to counteract what she saw as their undermining influence, Mother tightened her restrictions. Aunt Sophia and Uncle Irvin indulged us even more. Gischa and I were caught in the middle. It's a wonder we didn't get the bends from the sudden changes in "atmospheric" pressure.

Mother called us in every night at seven-thirty. Even in July and August, when it didn't get dark until 9 P.M! By eight we were lying in bed—wide awake—listening to the other kids singing and playing in the neighborhood. Boy were we mad!

"Mother is so *mean!*" said Gischa. "I bet she's the *meanest* mother in the whole world!"

"Yeah!" I'd pipe. "I bet she's our stepmother. A *real* mother wouldn't treat us like that!"

"I know, let's run away from home."

"Yeah," I agreed. "She'd probably be glad to be rid of us, anyway."

Sometimes, when the blistering heat made our brick row house uninhabitable, Mother relented. We became part of the gathering exodus streaming out of our stifling kitchens to catch a slightly less stifling breath of "fresh" air. Screen doors slammed with predictable regularity as kids ran back for forgotten skate keys, and fathers went in for extra chairs.

After supper on summer evenings, I could see Aunt Sophia and Uncle Irvin's rotund bodies bobbing toward me up the block.

"Hi there. How you-all doin'?" Uncle Irvin would call as he passed clusters of neighbors sitting on porches fanning themselves.

I remember one evening in particular. Gischa and I were slumped on the porch with the grown-ups. We were so hot we had no energy to play.

Uncle Irvin winked at me, then looked at my mother. "Request permission to take the troops out for ice cream, (smart salute) ma'm!"

Instantly we were on our feet, our listlessness forgotten. "Oh Please, please let us go!"

Mother's mouth was tight; she looked skeptical.

"Aw, c'mon Mary. We'll have them back by bedtime. I swear."

Mother agreed but she didn't look happy about it. She was probably too miserable from the heat to argue. Just to be on the safe side, I amscrayed out of calling distance, and waited for them at the corner.

Uncle Irvin caught up with me, and took my hand. We crossed the street taking a short cut through the alley. Aunt Sophia and Gischa followed a few paces behind. The tiny yards were bursting with bright red or pale yellow roses. I buried my nose down deep in their velvet petals.

"Watch out for bees and Japanese beetles honey, "Aunt Sophia warned automatically.

"She's all right, Soph. Let her be."

Laughing and chatting, we ambled past Bubby's, past the butcher's, past our school, and one more block to Diener's Drug Store.

Uncle Irvin pulled open the screen door. "Ahhh!" Cooler air fluttered down from the whirling blades on the ceiling. The long skinny strips of fly paper waved hello as we came in.

"Look!" I whispered to Gischa. "They look like raisins sticking up there."

"How ya doin', Doc?" Uncle Irvin hailed the pharmacist. He whisked me up, and deposited me safely on a round red soda fountain seat. My legs stuck straight out in front of me. Grasping the chrome edge of the formica

Eh-Heh-Heh-Heh-Chhemm!

counter, I kicked and spun myself around and around on my stool.

"Hey! Look at me everybody, I'm making a breeze!"

"Irv! Watch her, she'll fall!"

"She's all right Soph, I'm standing right beside her."

Now began a lengthy discussion of ice cream flavors, toppings, and the really big decision: should we get cups or cones? In answer to her repeated questions, Dr. Diener assured and reassured Aunt Sophia: "Everything is delicious—and the ice cream came in fresh today!"

Aunt Sophia turned to me. "They have chocolate, vanilla, rocky fudge, butter pecan, strawberry, and pistachio. What kind do you want, honey?"

"I want a vanilla sugar cone."

Aunt Sophia: "How about a sundae? Sundaes have hot fudge and cherries and nuts and whipped cream. Sundaes are delicious." Then after a pause, "Mother wouldn't know."

"I want a vanilla sugar cone."

"You hear that Irv? No wonder she's so thin. Tell her to get a sundae."

Uncle Irvin looked at me with his big blue eyes. "You want a sundae, honey?"

"I want a vanilla sugar cone."

"She wants a cone, Soph."

Aunt Sophia: "How about a nice chocolate milkshake? Milkshakes are good. It will make you fat!"

"I want a vanilla sugar cone."

Aunt Sophia (to the pharmacist): "Give her a vanilla sugar cone, but put lots of jimmies on it, hear?"

I really wanted that sundae. But Mother—I knew—had eyes in the back of her head. Sometimes she could even see through walls! I was lucky enough just to be here. *If I'm good, maybe she'll let me come again. Better not to push my luck.*

Poor Mother! I could see her sweltering on the lawn—swatting mosquitos, while I slurped ice cream under a giant fan. Nope. Definitely not a sundae! Some things were too rich even for my greedy little soul.

Aunt Sophia (to Gischa): "What do *you* want, honey?"

"A chocolate ice cream cone with jimmies." Aunt Sophia threw up her hands in exasperation, and ordered two hot fudge sundaes with all the trimmings for herself and Uncle Irvin. They ate slowly, savoring every mouthful. Uncle Irvin chatted quietly with Dr. Diener.

Aunt Sophia: "Ummm! Isn't this delicious? Want some, honey? Here, taste how good it is. Next time get the sundae—it's better for you, hear?"

We perched on our stools, our backs cooling off from the drafts of fresh air being pulled through the screen door. I licked my ice cream as fast as I could, but the sticky dribbles raced down my arm, and dripped off the end of my elbow. Uncle Irvin and Dr. Diener talked politics, but not with their usual enthusiasm. Aunt Sophia added her comments between mouthfuls of hot fudge and whipped cream.

Uncle Irvin finished his sundae and lit a cigarette. Aunt Sophia scraped at the last of the fudge with her spoon. I dipped my napkin in my water glass and scrubbed my sticky self as best I could. Then I slid off my stool and headed straight for the comics. Lucky Daddy wasn't here to see me.

"What do you read trash like that for?" he would say.

I had finished two *Archies,* and was deep in *Little Lulu* when Uncle Irvin called, "Time to go!"

"Goodnight Dr. Diener."

"Goodnight, Doc."

We walked out into the damp night air. Yuk! It was like walking face first into a line of wet wash. Uh-oh! It was almost dark. A tiny fist of fear clenched in the pit my stomach. We were late! Mother would be angry!

Aunt Sophia and Uncle Irvin laughed and talked as we strolled homeward. Didn't they know we were in danger? The closer we got to Mother, the quieter Gischa and I got. Just as we turned the corner on to our street—night fell! I moved closer to Uncle Irvin and reached up for his reassuring hand.

It was dark. Soft circles of light fell from the lamposts. The fiery end of a cigarette glowed. Lightning bugs flashed by me, flicking their taillights on and off. Easy for them, they didn't have to go home to Mother! I took a deep breath, filling my lungs with sweet honeysuckled air.

Aunt Sophia and Uncle Irvin stopped talking. All I heard was the sawing of crickets and the low murmur of people's voices as they chatted on their lawns. We were almost home. The fist in my stomach grew bigger. It was getting hard to breathe. We walked a little farther. Now there were only three more doors to go!

We moved into a circle of lamplight. A *loud grating* sound sliced through the heavy layers of moist air.

"Eh-heh-heh-heh ..."

Uncle Irvin and I froze. Our hands tightened. Electricity crackled around us.

"Chhemm!" exploded the final syllable. Uncle Irvin jumped as if he had been shot. I shuddered and felt the hair on the back of my neck stand up. A hush blanketed the neighborhood. Even the crickets stopped sawing. Uncle Irvin bent low and whispered in my ear.

"I guess I'm a little late getting you two back home. Don't you worry now, it's all my fault. I'll explain things to 'The Warden.' " He squared his shoulders and moved forward resolutely.

But I had heard the tremor in his voice. Tough as he was, even Uncle Irvin was afraid of Mother! It was the first time I'd realized that heroes could be human too!

Surprise!

Uncle Irvin may have had the body of a wrestler, but he had the makings of a poet in his soul. His generous frame encompassed an equally generous nature. If he had been a pot of soup, then Aunt Sophia would have been the ladle. She stirred his simmering emotions to such a fever of intensity they boiled over, escaping like steam into flights of passionate fancy.

For Valentine's Day he'd bring chocolates; three pounds of them in a satin-covered heart-shaped box. The card would be as large and lacy as the present, and bursting with flowers, cupids and doves. The message was always embarrasing and sentimental, but he knew that Aunt Sophia knew he meant every word.

For her birthday or their anniversary he'd give her a watch encrusted with tiny diamonds, or a pair of golden earrings and another incredible card. Those cards were Cecil B. deMillian in cost and in grandeur. Aunt Sophia always rewarded him by making a big fuss.

"Did you see what Irvin gave me for my birthday?" She'd jangle her latest piece of jewelry, and add, "And *look* at this *beautiful card!*" Everyone had to admire the latest present, then rave about the elegance of the card. Meanwhile, Uncle Irvin stood in the background blushing and smiling as he rocked his burly body from his heels to his toes.

His devotion to Aunt Sophia was so effervescent—it bubbled over like fine champagne and embraced me. I was part of his beloved, therefore I could do no wrong. Misbehaviors which my parents viewed as serious flaws in

Surprise!

my character, such as disobeying and talking back, Uncle Irvin dismissed with laughter and applause. He was my staunchest defender, and he never wavered. Not even when I gave him cause.

The summer I turned five, Uncle Irvin decided to give Aunt Sophia a surprise birthday party. Since she had never had one before, he wanted to make this one perfect. Mother agreed to let him have it in our basement.

"Everything's on me Mary, don't worry about a thing. I'll pick up some pretty paper plates and all, and order the cake."

Knowing what a mouth I had, Mother decided not to tell me about it. The first inkling I had was on Friday morning. Mother was scalding the chicken for *shabbes* when Uncle Irvin, carrying an enormous white bakery box, stopped in.

"I got the cake, Mary. Wait'll you see!" His face was bright red and shiny with perspiration. He cradled the box against his chest as if he were holding a beloved baby.

"Here, Irv," Mother directed as she preceded him into the dining room. "Put it down on the buffet."

With great tenderness he lowered the box, then lifted its lid with solemn reverence.

"What do you think, Mary?"

Mother leaned forward and caught her breath. "Oh Irv, it's beautiful! Soph will just love it!"

Uncle Irvin's chest swelled and his smile widened. If I had plugged him into a socket he would have lit up.

Hey! What's going on here? I wondered. I yanked on the corner of his jacket.

"Let me see!"

Swooping me up with an arm made of iron, he lifted me high above the box so I could see.

"Oooooh!" My eyes must have goggled like frog eyes. I'd never even imagined such a thing!

Rising before me like Everest, was a mountain of snowy icing. A border of creamy pink sugar roses nestled like little broody hens on top. Their plump rounded petals seemed to bulge with delicious promise. I could imagine the little pings of ecstacy as the soft blobs of sweetness slowly melted on my tongue.

With my finger poised above, I followed the dainty green vine as it twisted and curled around each luscious blossom. Sprouting candy leaves were so glossy, my teeth hurt just to look at them.

Shiny pink letters sprawled across the middle, but I was more interested in the tiny oriental bridge, and the two graceful swans. Even the sides of the mountain were decorated, lined from top to bottom with pearls that winked at me with a sly iridescent glimmer. This wasn't a cake—it was a fairy tale! For the first time in my life I was speechless.

I looked at Uncle Irvin. The blush on his chubby cheeks seemed to match the cotton-candy color of the roses. Mother was still hypnotized.

"They look so real," she gasped, pointing to the crown of flowers.

Uncle Irvin gave me a squeeze. "See, honey, this is a special surprise for Aunt Sophia's birthday tomorrow. We're not going to tell her anything about it. You think you can keep this secret—for me?"

All of a sudden Mother came to with a snap.

"Listen, Jo-Ann," she threatened in her scariest "you'd better listen to me" tone of voice. "You are not to say one word about this to Aunt Sophia, and if I find out you came anywhere near this cake, I'll punish you severely! Is that clear?"

"She won't tell—will you honey?"

"Na-uh," I said, shaking my head. Uncle Irvin lowered me to the floor looking relieved. He kissed Mother,

Surprise!

then me, took one last look at the cake, and headed back to work, whistling.

Fizzing with pent-up excitement, I took off. I had to tell somebody about that cake or I would *plotz!* But who? I paced up and down the back alley. Grownups were out, and Gischa probably knew already. I needed somebody my own age. Someone I could really impress.

Butzi! She was perfect! That cake was much too big for me to handle, but Butzi was twice my size. She could help. It wouldn't hurt to get on her good side either.

I ran across the alley and banged on her screen door.

"Hey Butzi, know what? We have something special at our house."

" Oh yeah? What?"

"It's a surprise birthday cake with roses and swans and jewels on it!"

"Let's see."

"Promise not to beat me up anymore?"

"Uh huh."

"O.K. But it's a secret. You have to promise not to tell."

"I promise. Let's go."

"Um, my mother's home right now. I'll come and get you when the coast's clear."

Now I had another problem. How could I smuggle Butzi into the house with Mother always watching?

Opportunity clip-clopped down the street later that very same morning. I had forgotten about the huckster. Every Friday the street A-rabs came on their horse-drawn farm wagons. Mother, like all the other women in the neighborhood, went out to squeeze the fruit.

As soon as she stepped out the front door, I flew out the back. I ran across the alley and fetched Butzi. On our way through the kitchen, we grabbed the step stool and dragged it into the dining room. In a flash I was up the steps, towering over the cake. I pulled the heavy box forward and lifted the lid. "Ta da! There, see? It's just like I told you."

"I can't see it," Butzi complained, straining to see over the high white edge of the cardboard.

"Stand on your tip-toes."

"I already am!"

What should we do? Victory was so close, but then—so was Mother. Through the open windows I heard the women murmuring in the street, the horse snorting and pawing, and the clank of the giant metal scale as the huckster weighed the produce. How much time did we have? Egged on by the sullen expression on Butzi's face, I made a quick and desperate decision.

"Help me lift it down—then you'll be able to see."

We each grabbed an end and pulled. The huge box lumbered toward us, inch by inch. I strained for the sound of Mother's shoe on the flagstone, ready to abandon ship at the first scrape. I didn't give a thought to Butzi. She'd have to plan her own escape.

What was that noise? Was that a footstep? "Pull harder, we don't have much time!" Whoops! The mighty box sailed right off the edge of the buffet, and seemed to hang for a second in mid-air. Like Jerry in the cartoons, when Tom chases him off a cliff.

"Catch it, quick!"

We flung out our arms and—oof!—it was like catching a two hundred pound gorilla.

The weight made the front part of my arms snap up. I staggered. The box fell against my chest, its sharp corner nipped the tender crease in my elbow.

I swayed on the top step of the footstool. *Don't* drop the box, I told myself, and *don't* lose your balance! Suddenly, the box tipped. I could feel my end lighten as the massive cake slid toward Butzi.

"Hold it up! Hold it up!" I yelled.

" I can't. It's too heavy!"

Surprise!

There was only one way to even it out. I reached behind me with my right foot, and backed down a step, still wrestling with my awkward burden.

One minute our arms were full of cake box, and the next minute—thud!—our arms were empty. For one terrible moment Butzi and I looked deep into each other's horror-stricken eyes. Then we both looked down at the floor.

The box had landed squarely on its broad bottom. Lucky for us the tuck-in lid had snapped shut.

"Quick," I yelped. "Help me put it back before my mother comes."

Butzi didn't speak but the panic in her eyes spoke volumes.

I jumped off the stool and grabbed my end of the box. Butzi grabbed her's. We heaved. The cake seemed to fly into the air then float gently back in place on the buffet—as if we were Wonder Women.

"Don't tell anybody," I hissed.

Butzi nodded and streaked out the back way banging the screen door behind her. I yanked the stool back to the kitchen, hit the screen while it was still vibrating, and zoomed down the alley like a rocket.

Mother had to call me three times for supper. As I edged my way through the kitchen, I searched her face for some sign. All I saw was her usual mealtime agitation. Maybe she wouldn't notice. Maybe I'd actually get away with it this time.

Saturday dawned warm and sunny. Another good day to play outside. Daddy bolted his breakfast as usual and crashed out the front door. Mother fussed with the food and the dishes. Except for nagging me to finish my oatmeal, she didn't say a word.

Uncle Irvin arrived around 10 in the morning. He and Zady had come to take me out for a drive. Good idea, I told myself. Then Uncle Irvin and I would both be away from the house till the party. *I know I don't deserve it God, but please, please, please let the cake be all right!*

I could tell Uncle Irvin was excited. His eyes were all sparkly, and his body looked swollen like Popeye's: the giant Thanksgiving Day balloon.

"Zady's waiting for you, honey. You can go on out to the car now."

I didn't wait for a second invitation. Ducking around Uncle Irvin, I flung open the wooden screen, and catapulted myself through the door. Suddenly that old Dodge, even with Zady's bulk filling the front seat, looked pretty reassuring.

I was halfway to the car when I heard my uncle's voice pronounce my doom.

"I'll just take one more look at the cake, Mary."

I leaped to the bottom of the flagstone steps and jumped onto the running board.

"I'm ready Zady, let's go!" *Maybe if we leave right this second I can still get away in time!*

My grandfather, unperturbed as usual, gestured toward the back seat.

"Get in da machine, Jo-Vennala, ve haf to vait for Urbin!"

Now I knew how Jimmy Cagney felt. I too was headed for "the chair." I climbed into the car. She was going to kill me for sure, but only if I let her. Scrunching myself into the corner farthest from the sidewalk, I tried to shrink into a tiny ball.

Zady, unaware that a bomb was about to go off, began to chat.

"Nu, Jo-Vennala? Vus machts-du?"

Didn't he know I was straining to listen? "F-fine Zady, how are you?"

The seconds ticked by. *What's taking so long? They must have found it already!* My body felt tighter than an

Surprise!

overwound clock. Suddenly a familiar voice crashed against my ear drums.

"Jo-Ann!"

My heart leaped into my mouth, and I bit my tongue.

Mother charged out of the house like an avenging Fury. Her eyes shot bullets, and her whole face worked. She flew down the stairs like a witch on a broomstick, and wrenched open the heavy back door.

"So help me God ..." she muttered through gritted teeth, as I huddled deeper into the corner trying to blend with the upholstery.

"Maren. Vus a da mer?" Zady demanded.

But Mother was beyond talking. She reached in with a hand of death and snatched me off the seat, as if I were a caterpiller she had found in the lettuce. I didn't touch ground till she deposited me in the dining room.

Uncle Irvin stood by the buffet. He looked shriveled like a Popeye balloon that's just been popped. I'd never seen his face so white. I started to cry.

Mother yanked me up to confront the evidence. **"What ... Did ... You ... Do ... Jo-Ann?"** She was still talking between clenched teeth.

I stared at the broken chunks of that once magnificent creation. It looked as though it had been hit by a bomb.

"I d-didn't m-mean to! I j-just wanted to s-show B-B-Butzi the cake—and it fell."

Uncle Irvin just stood there. He looked like he was going to cry too.

Mother lowered me to the floor. "Here, Irv. Here's five dollars."

Five dollars? Wait till Daddy finds out. Now I know he's gonna kill me.

"Go back to the bakery and ask them to make another cake. There's time."

Uncle Irvin came slowly out of his reverie. "Do you really think they can fix it, Mary?" Hope and doubt leap-frogged across his haggard face.

"I'm sure of it, Irv."

He sprang into action. Bending over, he gave me a quick hug, and kissed away my tears.

"Don't worry, honey, you didn't mean it." To Mother he said, "Don't punish her Mary, she's only a child. I know she didn't mean it." Then he grabbed the exploded cake and ran out the door.

Mother sent me to my room to think about what I had done. She said she wouldn't punish me because Uncle Irvin asked her not to. I languished on my bed for the rest of the afternoon. I didn't know whom I felt sorrier for, Uncle Irvin or me.

Just before dinner, I heard Uncle Irvin at the screen door. I crept down the stairs and peeked over the bannister. He was carrying another large bakery box. This time he looked more like himself. His color was better and he was smiling.

"Wait till you see, Mary, it's beautiful!"

With great ceremony he carried the new box into the dining room. Now they were around the corner and I couldn't see.

Mother drew in her breath. "Oh Irv, it's beautiful!"

I craned my neck around the bannister. "Can I see? Oops!"

Mother's voice sounded stern. "I thought I told you to wait in your room?"

"Aw, let her come down Mary."

Before she had a chance to argue, I was down. Mother pursed her lips and gave me the "I'm still angry, but I've decided not to kill you" eye and motioned me closer. When she lifted me up, I saw a white cake with yellow roses and matching letters. No Chinese bridge, no shiny pearls, no swans.

Surprise!

"What does it say?" I asked, trying to hide my disappointment.

Mother traced above the letters with her finger. "Happy Birthday Sophia, xoxoxo Irvin."

It was pretty, but it wasn't anything like the other one. There probably wasn't another cake like that in the whole world! Now Aunt Sophia would never see it, and it was all my fault. No punishment my Mother might think of could ever hurt as much as that.

I watched Uncle Irvin's face. Was he as disappointed as I was? He didn't look it. Neither did Mother. She didn't even threaten me this time. She must have realized she didn't have to.

Dinner was a little tense. Mother got all excited again when she explained to Daddy what happened.

"Five dollars? God sakes! Do you think money grows on trees?"

I sat with my head down and hardly ate any dinner. Daddy blew off steam at Mother, but he didn't say anything to me. After dinner Mother went down to the basement and set up the card table. Gischa and I arranged the cloth so it hung down evenly on all sides. Daddy cut some of his prized pink roses for the table, and Mother arranged them in the glass vase. Then we set out the pink and white paper plates, napkins, and cups that Uncle Irvin had bought.

Mother placed the substitute cake on a doily covered platter in the center of the table. She brought down a large pitcher of lemonade to which Daddy added a sprig of fresh mint from his garden. Next came the fruit bowl, piled high with well-washed apples, oranges and grapes, and the shiny metal nut bowl overflowing with almonds, walnuts, pecans and butternuts still in their shells.

When we were all finished, the table looked like a party. Now all we had to do was wait. My stomach tightened and fluttered with anticipation. Would Aunt Sophia *really* be surprised? Would she like the second cake? I still grieved for the first one.

Finally, The Family arrived.

"Happy Birthday, Happy Birthday," we called as Aunt Sophia moved down the steps after Bubby.

"Whose birthday is it? Whose? Mine?" she joked, winking and pointing to herself. Everyone exchanged kisses and hugs. Then Uncle Irvin led her over to the table.

"Here's your cake, Soph." He tried to pretend it was no big deal, but his voice shook.

Aunt Sophia clapped her hands with delight. "Oh, Irv, it's beautiful! Ma! Ma! *Gib a kick! Irvin koift, siz azay shane!*"

Bubby advanced to the table, and gazed at the cake in solemn wonder. "Ahhh! *Siz azay shane!*" she echoed, shaking her head in admiration.

One by one Aunt Sophia called us to admire it. "Isn't it beautiful? Uncle Irvin bought it," she said to me.

"She knew all about it, Soph." Uncle Irvin winked at me.

"You little monkey, you kept the secret! Kookle mookle from da dookle!" She tickled my tummy with her thumb.

"She almost ruined it ..." Mother began, but Uncle Irvin interrupted.

"She didn't mean it, Mary, she's just a child."

Of course Aunt Sophia had to know the whole story, so Mother told it, and didn't leave out a single word. I stood there listening—and "wishing I were six feet under," as Mother used to say.

When Mother got to the juicey part, Aunt Sophia interrupted. "She did? That little monkey!" Then she turned to Bubby. "Ma! *Herstu vus Jo-Ann hut getun?*"

Aunt Sophia chuckled and laughed as she repeated the story in Yiddish. Bubby clapped her palm to her cheek.

Surprise!

"*Vey is mir!*" But her eyes were dancing with merriment. This was just the kind of story Bubby loved.

Aunt Sophia fixed me with a mirthful blue eye.

"You'll never do that again, will you honey?"

I shook my head.

Uncle Irvin whisked me up in his arms. "Come on, honey, help Aunt Sophia blow out the candles."

He nestled me against his brawny body. I felt surrounded by his warmth and love. So what if I was a cake murderer? I was still Uncle Irvin's special girl.

It's a Boy!

Uncle Irvin fell in love with Aunt Sophia the first night he met her. As he later told his sister, Sarah, "I took one look, and that was it!" They got engaged when he was in the army, traveling through the country with the Quartermaster Motor Transport School.

Uncle Irvin hated being away from his sweetheart. He wrote passionate letters at least once a day and called her "person-to-person" whenever they stopped somewhere. At the end of each letter, he added this postscript: "Please say hello to Jo-Ann and Gischa for me and give them each a great big kiss." Gischa was six at the time, and I was a baby. He wasn't even in the family yet, but we were already high on his list.

Although they never had children together, they awaited each new nephew or niece as eagerly as if it were their own child, and greeted each new arrival with cymbals and drums. Sometimes Uncle Irvin was so moved he wrote poetry. Between his enormous capacity to love, and his incredible passion for Aunt Sophia, he embraced us all.

When, at the age of thirty-six, my mother discovered that she was "expecting" again, she was surprised and a little dismayed. Uncle Irvin couldn't have been happier! He and Aunt Sophia couldn't *wait* for the new baby! They spent the whole nine months catering to Mother's "condition." "Go ahead, you're eating for *two* now, Mary." They wanted to experience has much of her pregnancy as they could.

It's a Boy!

Mother went into labor early in the morning on the 19th of December. A terrible blizzard raged outside. Aunt Sophia picked Gischa and I up so Daddy could drive Mother to the hospital. We spent the day at Bubby's—listening to the wind whip the snow into submission—while we waited, and waited for news.

Aunt Sophia saw me staring through the vestibule window. "Boy! This is some blizzard! Isn't it honey? It looks like the end of the world!" She and Uncle Irvin were almost dancing with excitement. At the end of the hall was the breakfast room where Zady sat in his usual place at the head of the table eating cottage cheese. Nothing interfered with Zady's routine, not even the arrival of a new grandchild.

Bubby ran back and forth from the kitchen to the breakfast room. The more she worried, the faster she ran.

Gischa and I, Aunt Sophia and Uncle Irvin huddled together in the vestibule. We wanted to be close to the phone when Daddy called.

Aunt Sophia was fizzing with exhuberance. "What do *you* want, honey?" she asked my sister for the seven millionth time.

"A baby brother."

Gischa already had a sister, me. I guess she thought a brother would be an improvement!

"I want a baby brother too," I echoed, I was six years old, and I wanted to be twins with my eleven year old sister.

Uncle Irvin paced back and forth in the hall *kibbitzing* with Aunt Sophia. He was so full of electricity he gave off sparks. I knew they were trying to keep us entertained and distracted. It was too cold to play outside—and in the house there was nothing to do.

As the day dragged on the tension mounted. Every time the phone peeped, Uncle Irvin leaped like a mountain goat and grabbed it on the first ring. But it was never Daddy.

"Why is it taking so long?" I whined.

Only a few months earlier, Gischa had contracted infantile paralysis. She had been hospitalized for several weeks. The doctor told my mother, "*If* she lives—she'll make a complete recovery." *Baruch Hashem*, she did recover, but the memory of that terrifying time was still green. *Would Mother live and make a complete recovery— or would she die?* I was afraid to even ask. "Take it back, take it back!" Aunt Sophia would say. "Pooh, pooh, pooh!"

At five-thirty Bubby called us to the table, but my throat was so tight, I couldn't eat.

Every time the phone rang, Uncle Irvin whooshed out of his chair, and charged into the hallway, chanting, "It's a boy, it's a boy, it's a boy, it's a boy."

The rest of us sat frozen, straining to hear.

Each time he slogged back to the table, shoulders drooping. "It wasn't Kit."

After supper Bubby cleaned up the kitchen. Uncle Irvin listened for the phone, while Aunt Sophia got us ready for bed. Upstairs the extra room felt big and empty. The dim light made the windows black, and shadows danced on the ceiling, and walls.

In our flannel Doctor Denton's, and our cozy chenille robes, we sat on our cots and listened as Aunt Sophia told one of Bubby's true life dramas from Russia. Had things been normal, I would have been enthralled.

It was way past our bedtime when Aunt Sophia finished the story, but she didn't turn off the light. I jumped out of bed, and scooted across the long bare floor boards to the window.

"How deep is it now?" Gischa called.

"The glass is all blurry, I can't see." I rubbed at the moisture with my fingers. The glass felt cold and hard—like the fear in the pit of my stomach.

Wiping my wet hand on my robe, I pressed my nose and forehead against the window. "Hhuhh!" My eyes widened and I caught my breath. I was looking at an upside-

It's a Boy!

down snow globe. The sky looked thick and milky. Wind whipped the skittering snowflakes, churning them round and round in a creamy swirl. Huge monsters crouched in the glow of the street lights, nestled under their blankets of heavy snow.

"Ooooh!" I breathed, and the window clouded over. Where was our house, and Zady's car? Nothing was where it should have been this magical evening. Wasn't my Daddy *ever* going to call?

At nine o'clock the phone rang. Uncle Irvin shot up in the air like a rocket. "I got it!" he shouted, and rushed out on the landing chanting: "It's a boy, it's a boy, it's a boy, it's a boy, it's a boy."

Aunt Sophia and Gischa and I were right behind him. We watched him catapult his burly body down the entire flight of stairs. His feet hit the bottom, but his body kept moving, arching slowly forward over the bannister rail. He swooped the phone off the table with one hand, and whipped off the receiver with the other. "Mmmyello?" he sang.

Gischa, Aunt Sophia and I listened from the top of the stairs, our bodies tense as ironing boards.

"Who is it? Who is it?" we cried.

Uncle Irvin flipped himself off the railing and stood upright.

"Soph! It's a boy! Mary had a boy and he weighs nine pounds! *Nine* pounds! How about that?"

Thank you, God. Mother was all right! The cold hard fear was gone—disappeared like the steam on my window.

Aunt Sophia clapped her hands with joy.

"Hear that?" she said to Gischa and me. "You got what you wanted—a brand new baby brother."

She laughed with delight as she hugged and kissed us. "Ma!—Mammeh?" she bellowed as she went clattering down the stairs

I looked at Uncle Irvin. The light in his eyes was beyond joy. It was even beyond ecstasy. He was expanding so fast, I wondered if the small house could contain him. Maybe, like Alice in Wonderland, his arms and legs would escape through the windows and doors! He rocked back and forth in a reverie.

"Nine pounds—and *I'm* his godfather!" *Baruch Hashem,* Uncle Irvin finally had his boy!

Sixteen years later, on June 24, 1960, I was the one who gave birth. After a difficult, and protracted labor, I delivered my beautiful eight-and-a-half pound daughter, Melissa, *on Uncle Irvin's birthday!* Nobody could have given him a better present, he was so excited he glowed.

For several days I ran a high fever and was not permitted to have visitors other than my husband and parents. The Family chafed with worry and impatience. They weren't satisfied with telephone bulletins from Mother.

Bubby wrung her hands. "She's dead isn't she? She was doomed to die young. They shouldn't have named her for *Yusselle, aleva shalom*."

"What are you talking about, Ma? Mary says she's all right. She just has to rest a few days, that's all."

But Bubby didn't believe her. Finally they were permitted to come and see me. I could hear Aunt Sophia's voice from the other end of the hall. "Ma! Ma, where you running?"

Bubby appeared in the doorway clutching her big black pocketbook. Her face was solemn, as if, God forbid, she were making a shivah call. She hurried to my bed, grabbed my hand and kissed it. She gazed at me for a long moment, then turned to look at my daughter with tear-filled eyes. "Oyyy, Jo-vennala, she be beautiful! *Ken ahora!*"

Aunt Sophia's voice had gradually been increasing in volume. As it reached a *crescendo*, she walked in the door. Suddenly the room seemed smaller and sunnier.

"Boy, honey, you sure gave us some scare!" We were some worried about you, weren't we, Irv?"

Uncle Irvin loomed up behind her. "We sure were."

Aunt Sophia navigated around the furniture until she stood next to Bubby. She leaned toward me and peered in my face. "Are you all right now, honey? Are you all right?"

"I'm much better, Aunt Sophia, really."

"Ken ahora! You should live and be well—till a hundred and twenty years—and that goes for Miss Melissa, too. Bubby was so worried!"

She turned her attention to Melissa, whose big blue eyes were wide open, as if she were taking everything in.

"Irv, Irv, look what a *doll* she is—like Miss America, *ken ahora.*"

Uncle Irvin, who had draped himself in the doorway waiting for Aunt Sophia to finish, sauntered in.

"Nice goin', Doc," he muttered as he leaned over to kiss me. He tried to sound casual, but I heard the suppressed emotion in his voice.

He looked over at Melissa. "Well, would you look at that! Look at the *size* of her, Soph! She really is *some* doll!"

The three of them scrutinized every visible inch of my daughter's anatomy. They raved about her perfectly shaped head, her well-rounded body and her "healthy tan."

"Isn't she beautiful, *ken ahora?*" Aunt Sophia demanded of my roomate, Elaine, who had just had her own baby. "What did *you* have, honey? A little girl? That's nice." Uncle Irvin asked, "Did my niece Jo-Ann tell you that this baby, my *great* niece, was born on my birthday?"

The rest of the afternoon, whenever anyone set foot in our room, whether it was a doctor, nurse, orderly or a visitor for Elaine, each one *had* to admire Melissa and hear what a wonderful birthday present she had been.

The bell rang, but nobody—in my room—paid any attention. Eventually, the nurse came in.

"I'm very sorry, but visiting hours are over."

Aunt Sophia nudged Bubby who woke from her trance. After one more look at Melissa, she kissed me goodbye. Once more she assured me that my daughter would be beautiful, *ken ahora*. Then she headed for the door. Aunt Sophia and Uncle Irivn kissed me several times and moved slowly after her.

"Take care of yourself, honey, don't overdo anything, hear?"

"I won't, Aunt Sophia."

She walked a few more steps, then turned to face me. Uncle Irvin was right behind her.

"We love you."

"I love you too, Aunt Sophia."

When she reached the opposite side of the room, she turned once more. "Here's a big kiss for you and Melissa—smmack!"

"Hey Jo, I want to thank you for the neat birthday present. She's really some doll!"

"You're welcome, Uncle Irvin. Happy birthday."

"Thanks honey. Take care now, hear? We love you. Smack, smack, smack, smack, smack."

They both stood in the doorway throwing kisses, then reluctantly disappeared.

As their steps receded down the hallway, I heard the booming echo of Uncle Irvin's voice.

"...Eight-and-half pounds ...great-niece ...born on my birthday ...how about that!"

Turn, Turn, Turn

For fifteen years Uncle Irvin watched Aunt Sophia struggle. Armed with dedication and energy, she had battled not only Bubby's illness, but her own fear. Bubby tried to sabotage Aunt Sophia's efforts. She refused to eat. She refused to take her medicine. She *wanted* to die.

But Aunt Sophia couldn't let her.

For sixty-six years, since the day Aunt Sophia was born, mother and daughter were rarely separated. The last time was in 1940, when Aunt Sophia went on her honeymoon. From then on, whenever she and Uncle Irvin went *anywhere,* they always took Bubby. The two women stayed together in one room, while Uncle Irvin stayed in another.

When Bubby died in 1970, Uncle Irvin stepped in to fill her empty shoes. He knew, better than anyone, how Aunt Sophia was suffering. She had lost more than her mother and her child—she'd lost a vital piece of herself.

"Irv? Irv? What should I do, Irv?" became her frightened cry. Whom else would she lose? Her husband? A brother or sister? One of the *children*? God Forbid!

"I wish nothing will happen," she'd say again and again. "I wish we'll all be well."

With great tenderness, Uncle Irvin soothed and comforted her. "It's okay, Soph. Everying is okay."

"Say it!" she commanded.

"I did," he'd remind her. "Everything will be all right."

"I wish it will be all right," she'd repeat.

Automatically he would echo, "It will be all right."

More and more, she depended on her verbal amulets to assure her sense of well-being. Like a high wire supports a tightrope walker, they kept her from falling into the abyss.

The old litanies acquired a new urgency. They were no longer just an antidote to a compliment. Now they were necessary to keep the person alive!

If, when telling a story, Uncle Irvin forgot to use one of the magic words, she'd interrrupt him.

"Say *zi gezint*, say it!"

Uncle Irvin would repeat, *"Zi gezint!"* and then continue with his story until the next interruption.

If I said, "Can we come over to see you next Sunday?" she'd reply, "If we live and nothing happens."

She got so that if she excused herself to go to the bathroom, she'd say, "I'll be right back—if we live and nothing happens." Aunt Sophia had learned that the Fates were unpredictable. She was afraid to take anything for granted.

Except maybe Uncle Irvin. In their thirty years together she had learned how devoted and loyal he could be. During this terrible crisis in their lives, Uncle Irvin mourned with her. "How empty life is without that wise and wonderful little woman!" he remarked one day. He had expressed Aunt Sophia's exact feelings. Seeing him grieve comforted her.

Whatever they did, wherever they went, they were bombarded with memories. Together they cried, when they recalled Bubby's sufferings. But sometimes they laughed, and the laughter healed.

"Remember how Mommy used to take a pill?" Aunt Sophia asked for the fourteenth time. Uncle Irvin, blue eyes sparkling, picked up his cue.

"She couldn't swallow it because it was too big, so she took a piece of bread ..." Aunt Sophia made a circle the size of the bread with her fingers, "... and she spread it with jelly." Aunt Sophia spread the imaginary bread with imaginary jelly. "Then she put the pill in the middle," ...

now Aunt Sophia joined in ..."and swallowed the *whole* thing!" They both collapsed with laughter—as if they had never told this story before.

Each vivid recollection brought Bubby back to life, with all her warmth and humor, if only for a minute.

They appropriated her fractured English and used it in their daily lives. In restaurants, they ordered *Krice Krispies* and on the rare occasion that Uncle Irvin lost his temper, Aunt Sophia admonished, "Irvin, don't get so *coxited!*" A gleam of mischief in her eye.

Months passed. Uncle Irvin continued to feed Aunt Sophia with large helpings of love, patience and understanding. With his help she recovered her balance and resiliency. For the first time in thirty years they were alone together, with no major distractions. Within the restraints of a tight budget, they could indulge their passion for food, people, and politics. Not to mention the family. In spite of all they had been through, they were sweethearts still.

Three years after Bubby died, Uncle Irvin was attacked by two men he picked up in his cab. As strong as he was, he was no match for brass knuckles. He suffered serious head injuries and had to be hospitalized. Uncle Irvin was sure it was retaliation by the union. He had agitated against the gross corruption he saw.

Aunt Sophia had begged him, "Don't do it, it's dangerous!" But he couldn't go against his conscience, even to please her. Now he was hurt and couldn't work. She was sure they'd end up in the poorhouse. Aunt Sophia was frantic with worry and fear.

When he came home from the hospital he was still seeing double and was still unable to control his balance. In time, his vision returned to normal, but he struggled with the disequilibrium for the few short years he had left.

Throughout his ordeal, Uncle Irvin retained his buoyant nature by making jokes at his own expense. With humor, he could distract Aunt Sophia and deflect his own distress.

Eventually, he went back to work. He was able to drive without mishap, but he had to walk and turn very slowly; otherwise he would fall. Aunt Sophia became extremely tense. Her husband was no longer invincible. Now she must take care of *him,* instead!

Together they inched along, trying to live like normal people. They ate in restaurants; visited with famly. Uncle Irvin worked as often as he could.

Then, in 1975, he developed a cough. Aunt Sophia urged him to go to the doctor. "It's nothin', Soph, it's from the cigarettes." Finally, the cough got so bad, he *had* to go. The doctor ordered "tests," although I'm sure he knew what it was.

"I wish it will be nothing," Aunt Sophia pleaded fervently. "Please, God, let it be nothing!"

It wasn't "nothing." It was lung cancer. Aunt Sophia froze. She couldn't even pronounce the word. Nobody else was allowed to pronounce it, either. If you don't say it—it won't be true, right?

Denial became her religion for the next two years. She would admit that he was ill and needed treatment, but she insisted he would get well, "With our prayers and God's help." She even talked about his going back to work.

"He *has* to—so we can live like human beings." She talked about all the trips they would take and the things they would do, "when Uncle Irvin gets well."

Family members tried to reason with her, make her deal with the reality, but she was unreachable. This catastrophe simply wasn't happening. It was temporary, and would clear up soon—if everyone would just not *talk* about it!

Uncle Irvin knew his disease was terminal, he had to keep his own pain and terror to himself. She could not discuss a future that he would not be a part of. He had no choice but to collude.

Between hospitalizations, Uncle Irvin went back to work. He still struggled with his balance problems, and now the cancer too. He was tired and weak, and needed a cane to walk with. A cane! Like Zady! At the age of fifty-seven, he had become an old man. What a blow to his pride and vanity. He had always been so virile.

Throughout the operations, the chemotherapy and the medications, he remained cheerful and good-natured. He continued to take an avid interest in the family and kept in close touch with everyone, even those of us who were far away.

In March, 1976, the family had a brief respite from the pain of Uncle Irvin's illness, when my beautiful niece Jessica, *Ken ahora,* was born. Among the most enthusiastic celebrants were Aunt Sophia and Uncle Irvin. Another grand-niece! They were thrilled.

During that time Stanley and I and the children were on sabbatical in Palo Alto. In addition to letters, we exchanged audio tapes with the family, so we wouldn't feel so alone.

When my brother's tape arrived, there was also a message from Aunt Sophia and Uncle Irvin. I felt nervous about playing it, afraid to hear how awful their life had become. But, as usual, they surprised me.

Aunt Sophia: "Hi Jo-Annsky, Shmoogle-Poogle, remember? This is your old Aunt Sophia.

Hi Stanley and Missy and Sharon. I want to thank you all for your beautiful Valentines. We appreciated it. Thanks for not forgetting us."

I winced. Of course I forgot them, sometimes for days and weeks at a time. I was absorbed in my own new life, busy exploring the wonders of California. I loved them dearly, and I kept in touch, but I had no idea how tenuous their day-to-day life had become.

Aunt Sophia apologized for not writing:

"I'm up lots of nights with Uncle Irvin and I'm all broken up, but I'll try to write soon."

Suddenly, her voice took on a new animation and warmth.

"You should see the newcomer, Miss Jessica. Oh boy, is she a *doll* baby, *ken ahora*. She's adorable! The first time I saw her she looked right at me and gave me a big smile. You could just eat her up!"

Aunt Sophia went on to comment on how cold the weather was and how everything there was a "sheet of ice." She indicated how glad she was that we were all well and happy and living in such a beautiful place.

"Enjoy everything in good health and come home in good health! We love you and miss you very much!"

Her voice shifted down to a serious mode. I could hear her pain as she said, "Uncle Irvin's having a hard time. He's not well. Pray for him that he should be well. You all be well and happy and we hope we see you soon. Here's a great big kiss for all of you. Smack! Here's Uncle Irvin."

"Hi y'all, how've you been? Wait till you see Jessica. Boy, is she a doll! *Ken ahora.*"

He sounded just the same as always.

Aunt Sophia: Tell her *zi gezint*.
Uncle Irvin: *Zi gezint*, honey, and have a *gitte tzeit*.
Together: And *kimpt a hame gezint a haite*.
Uncle Irvin: Take care.
Aunt Sophia: So long.
Uncle Irvin: Here's a great big kiss for everybody, smack, smack, smack, smack!

How do they do that? I wondered. How do they put aside the terror of their own lives to celebrate ours? Thank God, we were able to give them so much pleasure. At this stage, they had very little else, except each other.

The last tape I have of them was recorded four months later. Uncle Irvin was back in the hospital. As usual, Aunt Sophia spoke first. As she talked, I heard intermittant percussive sounds which, at first, I didn't understand. They grew louder and louder. What are those terrible noises, I wondered irritably, as I struggled to listen. Then I realized. It was Uncle Irvin coughing. Those deep, gut-wrenching explosions were coming out of *him*. Each time he coughed, Aunt Sophia hesitated. Then resumed talking. Her voice sounded flustered and distracted, and she bore down **hard** on every word.

She began, "Hi Jo-Annsky," then proceeded to deliver a good natured ultimatum to our new puppy, Muffin. "... and stop aggravating my niece and don't do your business on the floor anymore!"

Abruptly she shifted gears.

"Last Friday, I'm sorry to tell you, I had to grab an ambulance and rush Uncle Irvin to the hospital. He was quite ill. You know he had to have half a lung taken out last year. Well, the tumor has grown back ... and they can't c-cut." Here her voice faltered for a moment.

"They're trying their best, with God's help, *and you pray* for us, hear? For *him*, that they will get rid of it with c-chemotherapy," again she faltered, "and that he'll come home *gezint a haite,* all better and all well, because I *need* him—*you* know—I have nobody else. We have no children. We have family, but you're in California, Mother is in Florida, Gischa is in Silver Spring. You know, I *need* him. You understand."

In a lighter tone, she said, "I pray you'll be able to settle in Palo Alto since you're so happy there, and I pray Uncle Irvin will get well so we can come out to visit you."

Uncle Irvin came on, his voice amazingly vibrant, and brimming with love. "I sure thank Momma and Daddy for you three kids! You've all been wonderful to us, just as if you've been our own. You couldn't *be* closer. I saw Larry on TV, he was doing an interview."

Aunt Sophia: "He looked like a regular professor!"

Uncle Irvin: Believe it or not, I'm bragging about him here in the hospital. I even brought the nurses in to see him. I told them, he's not only my nephew. *I'm* his Godfather!

Aunt Sophia: You know, honey, it seems funny to me that Larry has a little girl of his own. Remember just a couple of days ago—it seems like just a couple of days ago—you and Gischa were with Uncle Irvin and me at Bubby's?

Then she and Uncle Irvin recounted the whole story of the night Larry was born.

Aunt Sophia: And your daddy finally called and said, "It's a boy!"

Uncle Irvin: And *I'm* his Godfather!

Aunt Sophia: Such rejoicing! I'm sure that when the King's son was born there was rejoicing, but this was *more* rejoicing.

As they relived the past, their voices became light-hearted and happy. For a little while they forgot the trauma of the present; the uncertainty of the days to come.

Now that they were warmed up, they shifted into their crosstalk routine.

Aunt Sophia, prompting from the sidelines: We wish we'll be able to see Palo Alto—tell 'em, *tell* 'em!

Uncle Irvin: Aunt Sophia says we wish we'll be able to come out to see you one of these days.

Aunt Sophia: Tell her to pray for you, you should get well and maybe we'll move out to Palo Alto with them.

Uncle Irvin: Yeah, maybe one of these days I'll get well and come to see you in my old Tin Lizzie.

Aunt Sophia: Soon!

Uncle Irvin: Soon.

Aunt Sophia: No! We'll fly!

Uncle Irvin: All right, we'll fly. I'll use my wings and you'll use yours.

Aunt Sophia: And *we'll* live there too! Is there enough room for us?

Uncle Irvin: Sure, Palo Alto's got lots of room.
Aunt Sophia: Yeah?
Uncle Irvin: Sure
Aunt Sophia: (giggling) For a fat gal like me?
Uncle Irvin: Sure, we can live in the woods.
Aunt Sophia: In the where?
Uncle Irvin: In the woods.
Aunt Sophia: I don't want to live in the woods. (laughter)
Uncle Irvin: O.K. Jo, I want to say goodnight now. (Uncle Irvin was getting tired.)
Aunt Sophia: We love you *very* much.
Uncle Irvin: We love you very *very* much, I don't have to tell you that.
Aunt Sophia: Tell them—Say a prayer for me.
Uncle Irvin: Say a prayer for me.
Aunt Sophia: To get well.
Uncle Irvin: To get well.
Aunt Sophia: And we should all be together again, soon.
Uncle Irvin: Hope to all be together again soon. So long now.

The Last Valentine

After struggling heroically for more than two years, Uncle Irvin finally lost his battle with cancer. He died on February 14, 1977—Valentine's Day. How ironic—and cruel. He left Aunt Sophia on the very day he had always marked with extravagant reminders of his love. That year he left a different kind of reminder. Two days before he died, when he sensed that the end was near, he dictated a letter for Aunt Sophia to Ginny, my brother's wife. He instructed her to give it to Aunt Sophia after he was gone.

When the funeral was over, we all came back to their apartment to sit *shivah*. Ginny lured Aunt Sophia into the bedroom, away from the crowds of relatives. Gischa and I joined her to lend moral support.

"Here, Aunt Sophia." Ginny handed Aunt Sophia a sheet of white paper. "This is a letter Uncle Irvin left for you."

"He did?" Aunt Sophia looked dubious. "When did he write it?"

Ginny gently explained. "He was too weak to write and he wanted to leave you something. He asked me to give it to you after he died."

Aunt Sophia grasped the paper and stared at it dully. She couldn't seem to comprehend what she was holding.

"Read it to me," she urged Ginny, "*You* read it, honey. I can't see."

In a shaky voice, Ginny began:

The Last Valentine

February 12, 1977, Saturday, 2:45 p.m.

Dear Sophia,

I am asking Ginny to say these things to you as I am unable to do so. We both know that what I have is terminal and there is no hope, and that I will not be getting better. The tumor is growing inside of me and I know it is only a matter of time. I have spoken to the doctor and have told him that my only fear is of choking to death. He promised me that there are ways that he can prevent that and ease the pain and help me to die easier. I know, and you know, but it is impossible for us to talk about it.

I want you to know that I love you very much. I have loved you these past thirty-six years and am only sorry that I will not be here to spend our thirty-seventh together. I have never regretted asking you to marry me and am so grateful that you accepted my proposal. I have tried to provide for you and even though we lived beyond our means at times and got in over our heads we have always seemed to manage.

I have always put everything in your name and whatever I have left is yours also. I am sorry that I have to go before you as we have always done everything together. My one fear and wish is that we could do this together.

I love you very much. If I have been short with you of late it is only because of my frustration about not being able to be with you forever. I have spoken to several people and asked them to take care of you when I am gone. I tried so hard to get well for you but I have not been able to do it. It is not within my power. I am sorry to leave you alone, but please know that I never stopped loving you in all these years.

Don't mourn, go on living knowing that our separation will only be a temporary one and that we will be together again in another sense.

I love you so very much.
Love,
Irvin.

By the time Ginny finished reading, she and Gischa and I were all in tears. Aunt Sophia, who had been listening intently, stood transfixed. Her beautiful, usually animated face was frozen into a mask. She looked dazed, as if she had walked quickly through what she had thought was a doorway and instead had slammed into a brick wall.

"*He* said it?" she asked Ginny. "Uncle Irvin told you? You didn't make it up?"

Ginny patiently repeated her story and reassured Aunt Sophia that the letter had indeed come from Uncle Irvin.

Aunt Sophia took the letter and bustled into the living room. As she moved through the cluster of bewildered family and friends she demanded bitterly, "Did you see what Irvin left me? Did you see the *Valentine* I got *this* year?"

I winced at the pain in her voice. She was angry at Uncle Irvin! He had broken their emotional contract and left her all alone, wounded and vulnerable, with only a letter for comfort.

She turned to me. "What good is a letter?" she demanded. "I need Uncle Irvin!"

As the months went by she learned to live without him, but she never stopped missing him. She talked about him all the time. In her letters she'd remind me "You know Uncle Irvin (*aleva shalom*) loved you all very much. If he had lived, we would have flown out to visit you. *You* know that, honey."

Gradually, the terrible trauma of his illness receded and she could warm herself with happier memories. She began to read and reread the letter Uncle Irvin left her, finally able to extract some of the comfort he intended her to have. She shared it with me every time I came.

"Did you see what Uncle Irvin wrote to me before he died?" she'd ask.

"Yes, I did, Aunt Sophia. It's very beautiful."

"Read it, honey. Read it. He suffered so, poor thing."

So I would reread the letter, as if for the first time, to please her.

"Isn't it beautiful?" she'd ask, a wistful expression on her face.

"Beautiful, Aunt Sophia. I know that Uncle Irvin loved you very much."

At the end of the year of mourning, the famly gathered at the cemetery for the unveiling. The rabbi removed the cloth cover from the stone.

JASLOW
Feb. 14, 1977
IRVIN
MY MOST BELOVED
DEAREST HUSBAND
WITH ALL MY LOVE

Her final valentine to *him*. As usual she got to have the last word.

Eleven years later Aunt Sophia died.

She and Bubby were fervent believers in the after-life. They expected to be reunited with all their loved ones when they got to the next world. I would have to guess that since Aunt Sophia's arrival things have livened up considerably! She and Uncle Irvin must be regaling the angels with all the clever exploits of their beloved "children."

Bubby and Aunt Sophia also believed that those who died watched over and could even intercede for the ones left on earth. If that's true, then Aunt Sophia and Uncle Irvin know that in 1989, my grandson Jesse was born and that his

Hebrew name—*Ishai*—is for Uncle Irvin. He is the only child in the family to have that honor.

I can just hear my uncle as he struts up to the Archangel Gavriel. "Hey, Gav, how's 'bout tootin' a few notes for me? My niece Melissa gave birth to my great grand-nephew Ishai—and she named him after me!"

"Da Hell Mit!"

Der Schlechter

After barely escaping Russia with his life, and slaving one and a half years in a sweatshop to earn the money, Michael sent for Sarah. He was tired of boarding with his brother-in-law, and homesick for his own family. Here in the *goldene medine,* they would start a new life together. How could he know that what he saw as a beginning, his wife saw as an ending—an end to the only world she understood, or felt she could ever be a part of?

When Michael met Sarah at the boat, he found a pale woman, cold and withdrawn, who was so overcome with grief she couldn't look at him. *This is how a wife greets a faithful husband? All she talks about is her mother! Who did I marry here, a woman, or a crybaby?* His own mother died when he was a boy. He never spoke of her. If he felt any grief, he kept it to himself. *Women! Look what I went through to bring her here, does she even act glad to see me?*

Sarah was weak and sick. It was a hard trip for a woman. A man is built to withstand such hardship. Michael remembered what a nightmare his own journey had been. *Lucky I spent the extra money for the horse and wagon. She's too ill to walk to the new place. And so many baskets and boxes to carry! Her mother was very good to her. Now we have the bedding and dishes we need to set up our new home.*

If Michael expected Sarah to be pleased with the apartment he'd rented, he got a big surprise. She took one look, collapsed on the nearest box, and wept.

"How can I bring up a child in this filthy rat's nest? It's so dark! And the smell of chicken *drek* comes right up the stairs!"

Michael held out his arms to little Sophia, but she pushed him away, and burrowed deep into her mother's heaving breast. For six months Sarah refused even to unpack. Many years later she would tell Sophia, "If I'd had the money—I would have taken the first boat back."

Meanwhile Michael struggled with his own troubles. Making a living in this "land of opportunity" was not easy for an illiterate immigrant. All he had to offer was his determination to take care of his family, muscular shoulders, and a strong back.

Despite Sarah's melancholy, ten months after she arrived in Baltimore, she gave Michael his first son. *Yussel ben Michel ben Yakov Dov! Baruch Hashem!* A boy to carry on his family name. Fifteen months after Yussel came another baby. Michael named her Mariam in memory of his mother. Could he savor this child the way he'd savored her brother? Or was he thinking, *Nu? Another mouth for a man to feed!*

Michael moved his burgeoning family into a narrow apartment on Stiles Street. They had a kitchen and two bedrooms on the second floor. The only source of heat was the wood stove in the kitchen, and when somebody needed a "toilet," they had to go outdoors. All five of them slept in one bedroom so Michael could rent out the other. Then, three years later, Morris was born. Sarah nursed her new baby, but when she needed milk for the older children she had to steal a bottle off of the porch next door.

Michael was still slaving in the sweatshop when he joined the cloakmaker's union ...which promptly struck.

"Are you *meshiga?*" Sarah screamed at him. "Go back to work or we'll all starve!" But Michael refused to budge. "The unions are good for the workers," he shouted.

"If the unions are so good, then how come you've lost your job?"

When he could find nothing better he dug ditches, then worked as a blacksmith, but the pittance he earned was too small. Sarah felt ashamed that her husband would lower himself to such a menial position. She jibed at him. "This is a job for a religious Jew? A man who *davens* twice a day, and reads Hebrew?"

Sometimes he couldn't find work at all, no matter how hard he tried. "Gay gefin a job!" he would mutter with bitterness, after another long day's empty search. He paced the floor, puffing cigarette after cigarette as his trousers inched lower and lower over his skinny hips. Without lessening his stride, he'd flatten his elbows against his sides, pull up with his shoulders, and hoist his retreating gabardene back up to his waist. He must have looked like a large bird revving his wings for take-off—a take-off which would never occur. *A nother* exercise in futility—like his life!

It was humiliating to beg for help, but for Sarah it was easier than watching her children go hungry. She went to the wife of the wealthy sweatshop owner. To give herself extra courage she took little Mary along. *Mrs. Klavonsky has children...Maybe Mary's rosy cheeks and pretty blonde curls will soften her motherly heart.* Sarah spoke earnestly to Mrs. Klavonsky in Yiddish. The woman was gracious to Sarah, but her husband didn't give Michael back his job.

This is all Michel's fault! Does he have to be so stubborn, so hard—like the Czar? Oy, Mameh! How do I get him to listen? Tateh always listened to you. Dear Tateh, how I miss you. If only I could have married someone kind—like you!

der Schlechter

What could she do, leave him? With four small children, how would she live? *For this I had to leave my mother in Russia?*

Now when she spoke about Michael to her children she called him *der schlechter* instead of *di tateh*. "You think I wanted to marry him? He shouldn't live to see the light of another day!" Squeezing every drop of flavor out of her rich Yiddish vocabulary, she *grizhid* him at every turn.

Stung by his wife's fury, and bewildered by her disloyalty, Michael responded in kind. "What do you want from me Sura? It's not enough that I didn't desert you? A man works hard for a living. He wants *peace* in his home, and *respect* from his family! Is that too much to expect—after all I went through?"

When Morris was three Michael moved his family into a three story house on South Washington Street. It was a slightly better neighborhood. Conditions were still primitive, but now he had an extra front room. He rented out the top floor, and with the money bought a heavy second-hand flat iron and ironing board. With these he offered a "pressing and cleaning" service to the neighborhood.

Michael knew next to nothing about cleaning, but he knew an opportunity when he saw one. If a man came in with a spot on his jacket, Michael peered at the offending *shmutz* the way a doctor peers at an expiring patient. "You got a big job here," he'd say, his lips pursed. "I'll have to charge you extra." While the poor man waited and worried about the fate of his jacket, Michael took it back to the kitchen, and scraped it clean with his fingernail.

All through those years, Sarah complained to Sophia about Michael's harshness. Like his father before him, he ruled his household with an iron hand. Michael believed in the European concept of fatherhood. No matter what pain and humiliation a man suffered in the outside world, within the walls of his own home, that man was king!

Finances were strained in 1917 when Sarah discovered she was pregnant again. Just what she needed when she was almost forty—with her youngest seven, and her oldest fifteen! It was the time of the influenza epidemic. The pregnant woman across the street caught the flu—and died! Frantic with worry, Sarah went to the Associated Jewish Charities. They sent clothes for her children, and paid for medical care. Harry was the only one born in a hospital. She thanked God that she and her baby had been spared.

A weak man waits, but a strong man jumps at opportunities. All through these difficult years Michael worked hard, and kept his eyes open. When a friend offered him a "special deal" in 1923, Michael borrowed money and bought the house on Oakley Avenue. For the first time, they were out of the dirt and congestion of the city. They had an inside toilet, running water, and a two-story house that was heated clear through. Maybe the wheel was finally turning in his direction.

By now Sophia was in her early twenties. She worked full time, and gave her father every cent she made. Joe and Mary, who worked after school and on weekends, did the same. With their money, plus the little he'd saved from the boarders, Michael opened a "real" cleaning establishment on Ingleside Avenue. He hired a retired tailor from the Hebrew Home, called himself "The Link," and bought a second-hand truck. Joe drove the truck and Morris apprenticed to the tailor. As soon as Harry was old enough, Michael put him to work in the shop. It had taken almost fifty years, but Michael, the peasant from Karpilifka was on his way!

The next few years were the "boom times," as Morris would describe them later. They were the best the family had ever known. Sarah ordered new furniture for the front parlor, and every year Michael traded in for a new car. Four of his five children worked full time now, and whatever they earned they turned over to him. If one of them held anything back, Michael demanded, "Where's the money? This is not enough!"

"We need things, Pa!" the grown child would respond.

But Michael didn't agree. Weren't they under his roof? Then they owed him the money! They *wanted* to contribute, but they resented being bled.

In the spring of 1931 Mary got married and moved out of the house. The following October Joe suffered a complete nervous breakdown. He'd been having "problems" on and off since the age of twelve. Michael had to put his first born son in the state mental hospital. Sarah cried as if her heart would break. Whatever Michael felt, he didn't show.

Now Michael had two less pay checks to depend on, but he continued to spend. The pain in his arm was terrible. All those years of hefting those titanic irons had worn him down. He bought thousands of dollars worth of pressing equipment. *Sophia and Morris are working. I'll pay it off sometime.*

Then catastrophe struck. Three years after he entered the state hospital, Joe contracted pnuemonia. Before anyone could say good-bye to him, Joe—the bearer of the birthright, and everybody's favorite—was gone. The family froze, torn and bleeding, as if a bomb had gone off in their midst.

Sarah "cried plenty," as aunt Sophia later told me, but Michael didn't shed a tear.

Many years later my mother described the ride to the cemetery. "Aunt Sophia cried, but I couldn't. Zady just sat there. When Aunt Sophia began to talk about Joe, he warned, 'Soph'n! Soph'n!' to shut her up. I held it against him at the time. I thought he didn't care about Joe."

The family was already split. It had always been Sarah and the children against Michael. But this was worse. The impact of Joe's death rocked the family to its deepest foundations.

In 1938 Morris got married. Michael, still spending, sank deeper and deeper into debt. In his rage and frustration he demanded more and more from Sophia. *She* had to keep him going. It was a daughter's duty to keep her father afloat! But Sophia turned her back on him.

"No more money, Pa. Not another red penny!"

What kind of a daughter opens a mouth to her own father? I'm the boss in this family! I tell her what to do!

Without Sophia's help, he couldn't pay his creditors. He lost not only the business, but his self respect as well. From then on, it was Sophia who handled the family finances. More and more, Sarah relied on her.

Joe, *aleva shalom*, died in 1934. I was born four years later and named in his memory. The family was still struggling with their grief, their terrible outrage and loss. *Why? He was only twenty-seven! How could God allow such a thing?*

Bubby talked constantly about him. Again and again, she described how Zady, enraged by some trivial infraction, had backed poor Joe against the wall, and smacked him, *"anour in kup."* Her eyes filled with tears and her voice shook with anguish as she re-lived those painful moments. Before she even finished speaking, Aunt Sophia insisted, "It's true, honey, every word is true!"

Zady's behavior toward Joe had not been his only crime. Bubby often recounted how he made her beg for fifty cents, *every day,* so she could feed her hungry children. My mother, without realizing it, corroborated Bubby's story. Whenever I refused the "good food" she painstakingly prepared for me, she told me how often she'd been hungry as a girl. She'd say, "But if I complained to Zady, he said 'Hungry? What do *you* know about hunger? *Americanisher Kup!* When I was a boy in Russia, *I* knew hunger. My father said, 'You want something to eat? Then go out in the field and dig up an onion!' And's that's what I did!' "

der Schlechter

Each of them seemed to hold a grudge against Zady. Everytime I brought home a bad report card, mother reminded me how hard she had fought to remain in school.

"Who needs high school?" Zady had demanded. "A girl? Better you should go to work and help me pay the bills!"

Unlike me, my mother had loved school and wanted desperately to graduate. She hated the conditions they lived under, and wanted to better herself. I was less impressed with her words then with the violence behind them. Each time she told the story her voice choked with fury, and her hands clenched into fists.

I remember those early years of my childhood. Hitler wasn't the only dictator fighting for absolute power. My aunt and my grandfather had created their own war.

In 1940, when Uncle Irvin joined The Family's household, Aunt Sophia *really* took control. She moved Bubby out of Zady's bedroom, and gave her a room upstairs next to Irvin and her. By now Zady was in his late sixties. He was crippled with arthritis and could only roar. And roar. And roar!

Year after year he kept the whole family jumping. What was behind all the tumult? I didn't know. I only understood that *My Zady was a very powerful person!* Although I never saw a hint of his famous temper, the stories I heard, and his sinister appearance, were enough to give me pause.

When he sat, which was most of the time, he resembled a pile of old laundry. He didn't seem to have any bones—just flesh. The upper part of his body flowed right into the lower part. I was afraid he might one day ooze out of his chair like lava, and swallow everything in the room—including me.

His face was more frightening than his body. Pouches of loose skin hung from his jaws as if they were too heavy to stay on his cheeks where they belonged. Out of that sea of flesh glinted small yellow eyes, protected under a hood of wiry white eyebrows. The short curly hairs looked thick and sharp, like barbed wire. KEEP AWAY! warned those eyebrows. DANGER! warned those eyes. Needless to say, I kept my distance, and observed my grandfather with a wary eye.

I think Aunt Sophia was right when she said, "Joe's death almost wrecked our whole family!" She was talking about 1934, but I think the real damage occurred therafter. Bubby, and Joe's siblings, blamed themselves for what happened to him. Their burden of guilt became so great, they could no longer carry it. As if by pre-arrangement, they turned on the one person they knew was tough enough to endure the pain.

If You Can't Beat 'em, Outsmart 'em!

What Zady lacked in *gelt,* he made up for in *chutzpah.* He thought buying "on time" meant putting something over on his creditors. "They give you something for nothing? *Americanisher Kups!"* he would say. How could a lion of industry like himself have respect for such *narishkeit ?*

Then Aunt Sophia got tired of backing his get-rich-quick schemes with her hard-earned money and cut off his subsidies. When she pulled his financial plug, Zady's business dribbled right down the drain.

What kind of a daughter would betray her own father? And in his home, yet! Zady bristled with anger. In his Old World mind, this meant *war!*

In a last ditch attempt to hold on to his independence, he advertised as a driving instructor, but his one-man operation couldn't compete with the well-established schools. Zady didn't like being idle. His nimble brain grew restless. He had too much time to think ... and to plot .

Like any good General, Zady understood his enemy's capability. Routing Aunt Sophia, he knew, would require help. Behind Aunt Sophia's back, he blitzed the family with phone calls, complaining to relative after relative. Then he added my number to his roster. I had finally reached my majority. At least as far as Zady was concerned.

Riinnng!
"Hello?"
Silence. I listened to the static.

Then, "Heh, heh, heh." That laugh was unmistakable. My heart sank into my sneakers.

"Hello Zady," I ventured. *What now?*

Zady got right to the point. "Boobie is nervous," he announced, mispronouncing Bubby's name.

"Why is she nervous?" I was all innocence.

"Soph'n is nervous, and she makes Boobie nervous!"

I waited. I knew Zady hadn't called to report on the state of Bubby's nerves.

"Jo-Vennala," he demanded, as if he didn't already know the answer, "ven you married, you stayed in da house of your *fadder?*"

"Nnn-nooh ..." Suddenly, I saw what was coming.

"Dot's right!" he asserted, going in for the kill. "Ven you married, you moved *out!*"

I could hear the triumph in his voice, and imagine the glint of satisfaction in those crafty yellow eyes.

I waited for the clincher.

"Vy Soph'n don't move out?"

"I don't know, Zady."

"All da time she make Boobie nervous!" He massaged his normally gruff voice into a mixture of pity and righteous indignation, as though it saddened him to report such terrible injustice.

"What do you want *me* to do, Zady?"

"Bring schnapps!"

"Schnapps?" I was feeling a little dazed. *What did schnapps have to do with it?*

"If Boobie has schnapps," he assured me, "den she *von't* be nervous!"

He had zapped me again! *That's* what this whole *megilla* is about. *Zady* wanted schnapps, and probably didn't have the money to buy it. Poor old lion, I thought, bearded in his own den—and by his own daughter, *noch!* I wanted to help him, but the machinations of this Family were so complex, I was afraid to interfere.

If You Can't Beat 'em, Outsmart 'em!

Relatives weren't his only reinforcements. If we didn't give satisfaction, he turned to the Rabbi. Such a disrespectful daughter he had to endure at home! The Rabbi, much moved by Zady's *mayses*, reminded Aunt Sophia of God's fifth commandment. "Honor thy Father," he intoned.

The Rabbi could have saved his energy. Even Solomon couldn't have made peace between those two! Once either had embarked on a campaign, neither one could be diverted. Zady's cunning won him an occasional skirmish, but he was too old and disabled to win the war.

Then came the final insult. The DMV revoked his license. In one stroke, he had lost his income, and his mobility. Day after boring day he was left at home, while Aunt Sophia escorted Bubby on their appointed rounds.

Zady must have felt like a caged tiger, prowling the empty house, nursing his bitter resentment. *This time Sophia has gone too far! She needs to be taught a good lesson!* Deep within the recesses of his diabolical mind, he hatched a plan.

Late one evening, shortly before Aunt Sophia and Company were due to return from Johnson's, Zady secured the downstairs windows, and bolted the front door. Extinguishing the lights, he crouched in the darkened vestibule like a cat waiting to pounce. As soon as he heard the clink of Uncle Irvin's key in the lock, he picked up the telephone.

Zady recounted the story with such relish, I could see the blue flash of the squad car, hear the scream of the siren, and picture my uncle's purple face. Poor Uncle Irvin! How he must have lunged with frustration, his collapsed pompador beating against his forehead as his fists pounded against the unyielding door. He and Aunt Sophia must have bellowed like stevedores! From the other side of the glass, Zady watched, savoring the spectacle—his yellow eyes glinting with fiendish glee.

The police were treated to one of Zady's most convincing performances: his portrayal of The Fragile and Confused Old Cripple Abandoned by an Ungrateful Child. All that was missing were the violins wailing *Hearts and Flowers*. When Zady felt inspired, he could wring tears out of a stone!

He "made this trick on Aunt Sophia" several times, he proudly informed me, until the police learned to recognize his voice.

"Go back to sleep, Mr. Shapiro, nobody's breaking in on you," the officer replied firmly. But even that didn't stop my grandfather. The next time he called the fire department! Bubby's head and arm trembled worse than ever, but even schnapps wouldn't soothe her now.

Zady had "plenny more tricks" up his sleeve, and continued wreaking havoc no matter how much the family reprimanded him. When he wanted a massage, he waited cannily until Aunt Sophia and Bubby left for the day. Then he called the unsuspecting cleaning woman into his first floor bedroom.

Zady was pretty scary looking. I can imagine how startled she must have been. Motioning her to follow, he led the way to his bed, then pulled back the leg of his pajama. *Closer, come closer!* he gestured roughly, exposing his swollen limb.

He's after my virtue! the poor soul must have imagined. Grabbing her purse from the buffet, she fled.

When Aunt Sophia and Bubby returned, the house looked the same as when they had left it. Zady confirmed that the "girl" had left early, but somehow he forgot to explain why.

Every Friday the agency sent out a new cleaning lady, but after encountering Zady, not one would come back. Bubby and Aunt Sophia were beside themselves. They were running out of agencies, and they were living in a *shmutzadika* house!

If You Can't Beat 'em, Outsmart 'em!

Finally they got Marcella, which Bubby pronounced "Costello." She was a no-nonsense woman in her fifties who ignored Zady's "advances" and just cleaned the house. He couldn't afford a real masseuse, so he kept calling cleaning agencies till someone blew the whistle on him. Probably Costello.

When Aunt Sophia told the rest of us what Zady had been up to, our telephone wires sizzled back and forth for weeks. Zady's misbehaviors were like faults in our family's foundation. We were never sure when the next quake or aftershock would hit.

"Are you angry?" I asked him, thinking of his lost massages. Zady smiled his sardonic smile. His cat's eyes twinkled shrewdly.

"Da hell mit dem!" he roared—and with a disdainful flick of his gnarled wrist he dismissed not only the family, but the whole world.

The Driving Lesson

Daddy whipped the Ford into the parking space in his usual Kamikaze fashion, scraping the left front tire and hurtling me toward the door. I grabbed at the air in a convulsive effort to catch myself, but he braked sharply and my body snapped back.

"Zady will bring you home after the lesson," he bellowed, as the chassis heaved and the engine roared. I knew just how they felt!

I looked over at my father. Chin down, head thrust forward, he crouched over the steering column like a jockey. Even when he was still, he was not at rest.

His hand tightened around the throbbing shift stick making the veins on his lean brown arms pop out. Unlike me, he was rarin' to go. Unclenching my hand, I pried my fingers off the window.

"See you later," I mumbled, leaning toward him, and kissing his smooth cheek. I had a *feeling* about this day.

I oozed out of the car, and had just slammed the door behind me, when Varoom! He was gone—disappearing down the tree-lined street in a whoosh of exhaust.

I was alone, enveloped by the early morning quiet. How placid the brick row houses looked with their sleep-shaded windows, and their pregnant sun parlour bellies. *If I could count the hours I've spent here—how many years of my life would that be?*

I searched for my childhood landmark—the grey metal railing, then raised my eyes a little higher. There was

Zady *watching*. His vast image seemed to swell and shimmer in the sunlit glass door.

Waving, I started toward him. HALT! he mimed with an imperious thrust of his cane. I halted. Zady was as eloquent with his cane as Bubby was with her silences.

Squinting into the brightness of the reflected sun, I watched him maneuver his cumbersome body through the doorway, and drag his withered leg over the sill. He rested a moment on the landing, using his sturdy cane as ballast for his considerable weight.

His trousers were voluminous. The striped seersucker strained and puckered around his generous middle—like the skin of an overstuffed salami, then ballooned around his stumpy legs like sails. From where I stood, he resembled a cork in a bottle—rotund at the top, but foreshortened—as if his legs had been cut off at the knees.

Head down, he shuffled forward and teetered on the top step. I watched, breathless, as he pawed for the railing—in slow motion, as his trousers flapped. With deliberate cunning, he closed his swollen fingers around the grey metal lifeline—and stopped swaying. Woosh! I released my breath.

Step, scrape. Down he lumbered. Step, scrape. Rasping the soles of his shoes as he came. He looked so fierce with his eyes hooded, and his mouth clamped shut. The sun, glancing off his naked scalp, knighted his broad bent shoulders. But Zady didn't seem to feel it. His face was closed, like a fortress with its windows sealed and its drawbridge pulled up.

I ached to help him, but I didn't dare offer. I was afraid to move.

Finally, he gained the sidewalk. As he limped toward me, I noticed the angry patches of scale on his elbows, just below the hemmed sleeves of his freshly ironed shirt. I had forgotten about the psoriasis. For most of the year it was hidden under the three-piece suit he always wore. A golden chain stretched across his midriff like tiny lights across an expanse of bridge.

"Hi Zady," I murmured. *Was it all right to approach him?*

"Jo-vennala," he grunted. He stopped to let me kiss him, then shuffled past me toward the ancient green Dodge.

That car was older than I was. I remembered when Zady would sail up our street—at a majestic fifteen miles an hour. And in those days, and in that neighborhood—hardly anyone else owned a car. I'd watch till he got almost to my corner, then run like crazy, and leap on the running board.

The kids stopped playing just to watch me. For once, thanks to Zady, I was pretty hot stuff!

Once on board I'd assume a regal posture, smiling and nodding to my minions, like Elizabeth the First being barged up the Thames. Zady was so short, he hardly showed above the steering wheel, but I didn't mind. I'd smile at him through the open window and he'd grin back—my partner in crime. We both knew that if Mother ever caught us, she would *plotz!*

Now it was my turn to drive this behemoth, but at that moment, I would have gladly opted for the running board!

Following Zady to the car, I headed for the passenger's side, but no—he raised his cane again. Abashed, I climbed into the driver's seat. Zady hauled his girth in beside me, and handed me the keys. "Start da machine!" he barked.

My heart contracted with panic. What did he mean, "Start da machine?" I didn't know how to drive. That's what I'd come to him for!

I peered through the dust-covered windshield, stretching my neck to see over the knobs on the steering wheel. The car seemed to swell all around me. Like Pinocchio, I'd been swallowed by a whale. *I* couldn't control this unwieldy monster. Suppose I got us killed?

The Driving Lesson

I froze, but Zady zapped me, boring into me with those steely yellow eyes. He jabbed at the ignition with one claw-like finger. I turned the key and uttered a silent prayer.

The car thrummed to life with a lurch. Wildly I looked at Zady. He ignored my panic, and showed me how to shift into first. The car stalled. Again and again he took me through it, gesturing sharply, barking commands.

I repeated the litany: foot off brake, ease up clutch, push down gas. Coordination had never been my strong suit. Time after time the motor stalled. The morning was not particularly warm, but I was sweating.

Finally, like two recalcitrant lovers, the clutch and the gas engaged. The Dodge sprang forward with a little jump and rolled aimlessly between the cars lining both sides of the narrow avenue.

I struggled to breathe, but a herd of elephants seemed to be squatting on my chest. Inexorably the car moved forward. I sat there, unable to move, my hands frozen to the wheel. My mouth felt as if someone had inserted a hose and sucked out every drop of moisture, yet my clothing was saturated. Perspiration poured from apertures I didn't even know I had. *Dear God,* I prayed, *the Junior Prom is on Saturday, please don't let me crash!*

Zady sat beside me calm as pond water. Laconically, he raised a gnarled finger, and pointed where he wanted me to go. Ha! That was a good one! Did he think that *I* was in charge of this demon? Then why did it keep on nosing to the right, like a dog in search of a lampost?

A little more attentive now, Zady gestured sharply. I came to enough to yank the wheel, but I overcompensated. Now we were headed for the cars parked on the other side! Poor Zady! His rheumatic finger worked like a metronome. Right, left, right, left, as I struggled desperately to follow. Zig-zagging like a drunken dinosaur, we weaved our way along the street.

Finally, we made it to the corner. I hit the brake, and the motor died. *Vey iz mir!* Would this torment never end?

I started again with the clutch and the gas, but the lovers appeared to have quarreled. I couldn't get them to connect! In the meantime, a line of cars formed behind me. They began to toot. I was blocking the whole intersection! Sweat gushed from my armpits. My jaws ached. Evidently, the gears were not all I was grinding.

In the face of all this tumult, Zady remained cool, as relaxed as a pile of laundry. It took more than a few horns to arouse his ire!

Finally I got the darn thing started. Zady directed me around the block a few more times, till my lesson was over. Joyfully, I vacated the driver's seat. Knees shaking, I resumed my rightful position as a passenger. I was limp, as if my backbone had melted from the heat. The ride home proceeded in silence. Whatever our reasons, neither of us had anything to say.

A week later, although it was against my better judgment, I was back. This time Zady regarded me as a veteran, and took me further afield.

I actually began to enjoy it. Traffic was light at that time of the morning, and I was getting the hang of the steering pretty well. I still wasn't too hot on shifting. Everytime we got to a corner, I prayed—but the darn thing stalled anyway.

Week after week we went out, driving through the streets I remembered so vividly. Down Oakley to Pimlico, and around my old school. Past Uncle Dave's on Pembridge to the racetrack. Left on Chalgrove. I felt a stirring in my chest as I craned to look for the number. There it was, 5017—my old house! Every year during Preakness, we could hear the races being broadcast—and we didn't even need a radio. All we had to do was stand on the front porch and listen. *If only my old friends were still around ...*

The Driving Lesson

One morning I reported for duty as usual. I noticed a kind of glitter in Zady's eye. *Uh-oh!* I should have warned myself. *Be careful!* But I was too full of myself to heed.

Before I knew it, he had me in heavy traffic, on roads I had never even *seen*. Something fluttered slightly in my stomach. A tiny tendril of fear began to sprout. Where in the world could we be going? Had I been with anyone else, I would have asked.

All of a sudden Zady gestured. *"Daw!"* he commanded, pointing to a wide concrete driveway. I turned in and advanced on a low brick building. From a pole at the front waved a large American flag. *Maryland State Department of Motor Vehicles,* read the sign.

My heart dropped into my stomach the way a guillotined head drops into the basket. "Zady," I cried. "What are you doing? I'm not ready!" But Zady had apparently gone deaf, like the proverbial adder. The hoods came down over his eyes, and his face, despite the layers of loose flesh, looked sharp—like a hatchet. Ignoring my wails of anguish, he motioned me into the waiting line. I glanced at the car in front of me. *Easy Method Driving Academy,* it read. Oh God, I thought, why couldn't I have taken lessons from a *real* teacher—like any normal person?

Tortoiselike, we crawled forward. My fingers wound around the steering wheel like ivy. My biceps tightened into knots.

From the corner of my eye I watched Zady. He pulled his wallet out of his pocket, and extracted a crisp five dollar bill. With great deliberation, he opened a booklet he was holding and inserted the bill between the pages, making sure the denomination showed. Settling his body back against the cushion, he smiled craftily and commenced to wait.

Gevalt! I thought. Wasn't I in enough trouble already? Did he want me in jail as well? Every minute we were inching closer. Any second now my fate would be sealed!

I sat there entombed in my own misery. Suddenly the sun went out as a tall shadow loomed beside me. Were we having an eclipse? No, this shadow had a uniform, not to mention a machine-gun voice.

"Name!" snapped the uniform, but I was light years beyond answering. If the tongue is really the pen of the heart, then I seemed to have run out of ink!

Ignoring my catatonia, Zady leaned across me with surprising agility, and proferred the tainted booklet. "Is *dis* vat you vant?" he inquired silkily—and winked!

I was afraid to look at the officer, so I stared at Zady's hand. The skin looked dry and pruney, as if he had left it too long under water. The policeman opened the booklet. I held my breath.

Smooth as honey, the man slipped the money out of the booklet and into his pocket. Then he scribbled something on his clipboard. That's it, I thought. I'm doomed!

Without speaking he climbed into the back seat. Ready or not, the test had begun. Zady sat beside me in silence as the gestapo ordered me through my paces. After each badly-executed manuever, the man jotted something on his clipboard. His face was hard, his eyes like marbles. I struggled to contain my tears.

I felt like I'd been born sitting behind that wheel, but finally, my exam was over. Zady waited, inscrutable as ever, while my tormentor tallied my score. I just sat there chewing my lip, too done in to even pray for Intervention.

With a face like death, the man handed me my papers. I closed my eyes. I wasn't ready for the verdict. Taking a deep breath, I dredged up my last fragment of courage. After all, what more did I have to lose?

I sneaked a look—and a single word leaped out at me. "Passed," screamed the big black letters. *"Passed!"* I couldn't believe it!

My insides went all billowy, as if someone had been stirring them up with a whisk. I knew I hadn't earned that grade—but at least we hadn't been arrested! The best part was, I didn't have to drive with Zady anymore.

Feeling a little guilty, I peeked at my grandfather. His face was impassive, but his eye definitely glittered under his heavy lid. I waited. Almost imperceptibly I saw his lips twitch. Then his mouth turned upwards into a sly grin. I said nothing, just waited for my instructions. Zady didn't disappoint me. "*Nu,* Jo-vennala?" he said, gesturing toward the horizon. "*Mir gaen.* Start da machine!"

The Lion and the Mouse

"Zady's in the hospital," Mother informed me. Her voice over the long-distance wire was even, matter-of-fact, as if she were delivering The Evening News. "He's pretty sick," she added.

"Zady? In the hospital?" *How can that be? Zady's invincible—everybody knows that.* For as long as I could remember, he had loomed over the family horizon, ominous and unpredictable, threatening to destroy our equilibrium the way a thunder cloud threatens the peace and sunshine of a summer's day.

Mother interrupted my reverie, practical as always. "When you come in for Thanksgiving, you can visit him. It may be your last opportunity."

My stomach lurched. Impossible! Zady was a *force* in the universe, like gravity. Elemental forces don't evaporate, they impinge. It's their nature. *What will happen to The Family?*

Several times over the next two weeks I tried to picture my grandfather, sick and dying, but I couldn't do it. The only image I could conjure was the one I'd carried since childhood of the MGM lion.

How well I remembered those Saturday matinees: I sat frozen in my seat clutching the armrests in anticipation. Any minute now...here it comes...the snap of the mighty head, the flash of the cavernous jaws, the gleam of the steely eyes narrow with cunning. I held my breath waiting for the thunderous roar that would explode against my eardrums.

This is the Zady I had in mind when finally, on the last day of my visit, I made myself go to the hospital. As I pulled into the circular driveway, I craned up at the familiar red brick building. *Five years since the last time...only then I was in labor with Missy.* I waited for the warm feelings of pleasure to bubble through me, but even the memory of that exciting, special morning gave no comfort. All I felt was cold dread, massing against my insides like a mountain of solid ice.

My chest tightened as I stepped off the elevator. *Why are hospital corridors so interminable?* Eyes front, I moved past the open doorways—looking at the numbers, not the bodies languishing inside. I felt like a character in a Forties melodrama—*Susan Hayward?*—searching for a room I didn't want to find.

There it is on the corner, number two-sixty-eight. Here goes. Taking a deep breath, I peeked around the door frame. *That couldn't be Zady ... must be the wrong room.* I glanced at the name chart. *Michael Shapiro. My God, it was him!*

Zady lay like a shipwrecked hulk becalmed in a sea of white linen. Dwarfed by the vastness of his pillow, his once massive head looked naked, shriveled—like a dessicated melon. Against the hollows of his jaundiced cheeks, his acquiline nose had sharpened into a beak. His eyes were closed, hooded, leaving his face unguarded. *Vulnerable.* That face which had seemed so terrifying when it was corpulent, had become heartbreaking in its emaciation.

I tip-toed closer. "Hello, Zady." More like a murmur, than a salutation.

His eyes opened slowly. They were like tunnels, dark with pain. "Jo-vennala." A tiny flash of humor lit the darkness. The corners of his mouth turned up. "*Nu* Jo-vennala? *Vus machts-du?*"

I began to talk, faster and faster. Missy's escapades in kindergarten, Sharon's vocabulary, so accelerated for a two year old, Stanley's academic triumphs. Zady listened, struggling to concentrate.

He closed his eyes. I wound to a stop. *Is he sleeping? His lips look so bruised and swollen.* I leaned closer. "Do you need anything, Zady?"

He screwed up his face. "Hoits me," he grunted, then gestured vaguely, "da leg."

"What should I do?"

"Get da noice...rub da leg."

"I'll be right back." *Thank God I have something to do!* I charged down the hallway to the nurse's station. "My grandfather's in a lot of pain," I blurted. "He needs somebody to rub his leg."

The young blonde nurse eyed me with a sour expression. "We don't rub legs," she whined.

For a minute, I was speechless. *Isn't this a hospital?* "What do you mean you don't rub legs?"

"We just don't, that's all." She busied herself with her clipboard.

"But the man is in pain! Suppose he were *your* grandfather?"

"We don't rub legs." She refused to look at me.

My jaw clenched. *Bubby's right. Never ever go to a hospital. They only make you sicker!* With fists swinging, I marched back to my grandfather.

"Nu, Jo-Vennala?" He sounded weaker—the spark of humor had gone from his eyes.

"She won't come Zady. I don't know why. Show *me* where it hurts. *I'll* rub it for you."

His leg was like ice, the skin dry and scaley. I rubbed hard, trying to warm him up. I knew a little about leg cramps from childhood. My hands ached, but I massaged on. "How's this Sade?" Spontaneously I'd used his pet name, the one my brother had coined before he could pronounce his Z's.

"*Git*, Jo-Vennala, *git. A dank.*"

I rubbed until the bell rang. Visiting hours were over. "Good-bye, Zady." I kissed his yellowed cheek. *Will I ever see him again?*

The next day I flew back to Rochester, to my own family. Before I knew it, I was immersed in the daily grind. Weeks passed. Mother reported no progress in Zady's condition. His image grew dimmer and dimmer, receding to the back of my conscious mind.

Then, at the end of December, the call came.

"Zady's gone, Jo-Ann."

Why don't I feel anything? "When is the funeral?"

"He was buried last Tuesday."

"What? Why didn't you *tell* me?"

"Because I knew you couldn't fly in again so soon, and I didn't want you to feel guilty."

I do feel guilty. I'm relieved that I didn't have to go. Am I unnatural?

"Zady was very grateful for your visit. He said that after you came, he got much more attention from the nurses. He said, "She takes after me. She knows the way to get things done!"

A drop of warmth rose inside me, expanding with the bouyancy of a soap bubble. I felt like the mouse in the fable. For a short time, at least, I had eased the throb of the lion's paw. It had taken twenty-seven years, but I had finally done a *mitzvah* for my grandfather.

Redemption

One advantage in living a long time is that it gives us the leisure to deepen our understanding, and expand our perceptions of events that occurred many years before. It has taken Michael's children a lifetime to overcome their anger, but they have finally forgiven him.

Seventeen years after Zady died, when Aunt Sophia was in her eighties, she had this to say about her father: "He wasn't lazy, he was *never* lazy. There were times you couldn't *buy* a job."

She went on to describe his arrival in this country in her own inimitable way. "So what do you do with a greenhorn? He can't read, he can't speak the language, he can't write. You stick him in a shop on the third floor, and you give him a twelve pound iron and you say 'press'—in the heat and in the cold, and on starvation wages!"

That remark reminded me of an incident from my childhood. A hobo had come to our house begging, and my mother, incensed, had banged the door in his stubbly face.

"Why didn't you give him anything?" I asked.

"Why should I Jo-Ann? That man had two healthy legs. Zady is a cripple. If Zady can work for a living, why can't he?"

My mother's words were a revelation to me. At that moment, I felt proud of my Zady. How had I come to forget that?

Later in that same conversation, Aunt Sophia said something very poignant. "Zady was *very* Orthodox. He had *never* worked on *Shabbes*. But in this country, at that time, either you worked on Saturday—or you didn't work. His family was growing, he had to make a living. The first Saturday he had to work, he came home, put his head on the table and cried like a baby. It broke his heart that he should have to work on *Shabbes*."

I heard the catch in Aunt Sophia's voice—as if it broke her heart to tell about it.

She continued. "Zady had terrible pain in his leg from his arthritis. He'd get in a hot tub about twenty-five times a day and stay there as long as he could. But it only gave him relief for a few minutes. He would be stting at the table eating, and the pain would hit him so hard! He'd jump up and stand to eat. Then it would get so bad, he'd throw all the food down and run to the tub. He had excruciating pain all the time."

Wouldn't Zady be pleased, I thought, to hear his daughter acknowledge him? Especially *this* daughter. He would have been shocked!

Six years later, when we had gathered after Aunt Sophia's funeral, I asked Uncle Morris and Uncle Harry to describe their father.

Morris said, "He was a nice guy, but a tough guy, see what I mean? He came from Russia."

He thought a moment, then added, "He was short—but a giant in his character."

"Do you remember Zady hitting you with the strap?" I asked.

"Sure, I do, but I deserved it. That's how bad of a kid I was."

Morris told this story to prove his point. "One day, the family was sitting at the table. Joe said something to me that I didn't like, so I picked up an apple and threw it at his head.

Joe ducked and the apple went right through the plate glass window."

Morris paused for dramatic effect, then continued.

"That was the end of me. I knew it was time to *go* 'cause my father gave me the *bad* eye. He stood up ready to grab me. I ran through the front door and kept on running. If I hadn't, he would've grabbed my ear, and turned it three quarters of the way around. When he did that my ear would hurt for months. That was *worse* than the strap. I'd laugh, but it hurt like hell!" Morris chuckled. His eyes sparkled with devilment. He was relishing every word.

Me: "Weren't you afraid to come home?"

Morris: "Nah, Zady got hot fast, but he cooled off fast too."

Harry: "That's 'cause Bubby would say 'Cool off!' "

Harry added, "Zady was aggressive, he always pressed forward. He raised the level of the family. He took us from the slums to the suburbs, with never a backward move. Some people called him tyrannical, but I call him aggressive."

Morris: "He didn't drink or run around. He worked hard all the time."

Suddenly I remembered a comment from an earlier conversation. My mother had been talking about how often Bubby complained to her about Zady, and how she'd had to listen to a long list of grievous injustices. My mother-to-be was still living at home at the time. She was tired of this ancient litany. In exasperation she had burst out, "So why don't you leave him, Ma? We can manage. The charities will help us."

Bubby had fixed her younger daughter with a reproachful eye. "So what is he—a lay-a-bout? A gambler?" she demanded. "Why should I leave him? *Americanisher Kup!*"

My mother, exhausted from my intense and persistent questions, put it this way, "Zady did the best he could according to his culture. We all did. He loved Bubby and all the children and tried to make a home for us."

I think that's true.

Zady's image continues to appear unsummoned in my mind. But beetles no longer skitter down my spine, and his eye no longer strikes me as sinister.

I dreamed about a lion the other night, only this time he didn't roar—he smiled.

Bashert Iz Bashert!

As I write these words, I am sitting in my sunny new office—on Bubby's Victorian couch—the same couch that graced her front parlour on Oakley Avenue so many years ago. In those days no one *sat* on the couch. We merely admired its rose-quilted splendor from the doorway.

I remember tip-toeing into that room when no one was looking, just to stare more closely at what I fancied to be...a Lovely Lady. The atmosphere was as dark and hushed as a museum. Sunlight, like an unfaithful lover, had been banished from the room—lest he unwittingly damage the Lady's finery. I felt humbled by her dignity, as though I were in the presence of royalty.

When The Family sold the house in 1967, and moved into a small apartment, the "good" couch was demoted to everyday status. Their new life no longer embodied the grandeur of a front parlour. The dainty material, never intended for daily use, began to wear. It survived Bubby's death in 1970, and, faded and frayed, survived Uncle Irvin's five years later. After that, it just gave way.

Large tears appeared in the fabric, exposing blobs of coarse yellowed stuffing. Once released, they oozed and swelled out of every aperture. The Lovely Lady had fallen into disarray. Her joints creaked and her springs lost their bounce. Her bottom sagged almost to the floor. She was fatigued, too tired to provide either support or comfort.

Some of us stepped in and had her resurrected. New springs were installed and her frame was reinforced and strengthened. Aunt Sophia chose a sturdy cream-colored fabric strewn with gold and orange flowers to re-cover her. When the couch was finished it looked quite attractive. It just wasn't Bubby's anymore.

For me, the original couch and Bubby had been inextricably entwined. One reminded me of the other. Both *appeared* to be pale and delicate, standing demurely in the background. Yet, it's presence had dominated that room, just as Bubby's presence had dominated the family. It was as if that couch, as a consequence of living with her all those years, had somehow absorbed Bubby's spirit. Toward the end of her life, when she got so sick, Bubby too had sagged, but—like the couch—she stayed on her feet, bruised but unbeaten.

In time, I got used to the "new" couch. Over the next eleven years, it became Aunt Sophia's. Its curvaceous body widened at the seat and shortened at the leg, just as hers did. Its sensuous well-padded back promised softness and comfort, enticing me to snuggle close against it. Even the blonde highlights in the fabric mirrored Aunt Sophia's golden hair.

When Aunt Sophia died without leaving a will, the family had a dilemma. What should we do with her things? The small personal items were easy to divide; each of us took what we found most meaningful. But the couch was another matter. Everyone wanted to keep it in the family, but nobody had room to house it!

Finally, my brother Larry agreed to take it, "temporarily." That was three years ago.

I never dreamed I'd ever own that couch. I live three thousand miles away. How could *I* take it? Someone else would volunteer, I told myself. Someone *had* to.

At the end of November, Stanley and I flew back to Baltimore for a long reunion weekend. After a pleasant afternoon with the family, we all gathered at Larry's for dinner and the evening. Aunt Sophia's couch, solid and familiar, occupied the main wall of the living room. From that vantage point one commanded the best and most comprehensive view of the entire room. How appropriate, I thought, for Aunt Sophia to be represented at a family gathering. And, of course, she's right in the middle, as usual.

I nestled into an ample corner of the couch and allowed its healing aura to permeate me. "I *love* sitting on this couch!" I exclaimed to no one in particular. "It feels so good!"

"Enjoy it while you can," Larry responded. "This may be your last opportunity. I'm planning to sell it."

He's joking. He can't possibly mean it. But when I looked into his normally warm hazel eyes I saw no spark of humor.

"I already have a potential customer," Larry continued. "He saw it a few days ago. He'll be calling to let me know."

I was unprepared for the intense rush of pain that welled up in me. I leaped to my feet and moved quickly toward the kitchen, ashamed of the tears spilling down my cheeks. It was like losing Aunt Sophia all over again. Pictures began to flash through my mind, snapshots of all the relatives who had shared that couch with Aunt Sophia over the years.

With a pang, I remembered sitting there with Uncle Irvin who was home for a brief respite from the hospital. He looked thin and disheveled in his pajamas and robe. Embarassed by his appearance, he darted his fingers through what was left of his once luxurious pompador. "I guess I don't have much left," he offered ruefully. "It's from the chemo." The next time I came was for his funeral.

As soon as I got control of my voice, I whirled on my brother. "You're going to *sell* Aunt Sophia's couch—that's been part of the family forever? It's older than I am! How can you even *think* of such a thing?"

Larry's voice was calm and even. "I understand how you feel, and I'm sorry. If you or someone else in the family can take it, fine. Otherwise I have to get rid of it. I have no choice."

I knew that tone in his voice. *He is absolutely serious; he's not going to budge an inch!* Mentally I reviewed the possibilities, but it was hard to think with such a heavy weight on my chest. *Maybe we could ship it cross-country. How? In a van? Truck? Train? That would probably cost a fortune. But, what if we could afford it...where would we put it?* I panned quickly through the six small rooms in my home. Every one was filled. It was impossible! *But, if we don't take it, some stranger will. We have to take it! Maybe the garage...or the shed?* One thought chased another through my mind the way a cat chases its tail. I was getting nowhere.

Stanley saw the pain in my face and understood my anguish. He missed Aunt Sophia too. He knew how much everything concerning The Family meant to me. "Where could we put it?" he wondered out loud. "Larry, do you have a yardstick?"

The tension was shattered by sudden activity as my sweet husband and my hopeful brother paced off the measurements. Stanley sketched out rough calculations. A tiny bud of hope began to blossom in my constricted chest. Could we do it? *Oh please, please, let us do it!* I focused all my concentration and *willed* us to succeed. Finally Stanley spoke. "If we move some of the bookcases, we can put it in your office."

In the morning, I could hardly wait to call the trucking company. Now that my dream was almost a reality I was afraid some twist of fate would steal it from my grasp. Shades of Bubby's Evil Eye. The cost turned out to be quite reasonable. I made all the necessary arrangements, then called my brother at work. "I'm taking it, it's definite. Tell your customer you changed your mind," I crowed.

Larry laughed. "I haven't heard from him. He probably didn't want it anyway."

As soon as we returned to San Diego we attacked my office.

"What if we put the desk over here and the couch over there?"

"That won't work."

"O.K., let's put the bookcases on this wall and the couch under the window."

"Then there's no room for the desk!"

Round and round we went. Oh God, I thought, the couch is on its way. Suppose we really don't have room? Tentacles of panic squeezed my gut. Finally, in a burst of brilliance, Stanley devised a solution.

"Since there's so much unused space near the ceiling, we can run a shelf all around the top of the room and put the books you don't use up there. That will empty one whole bookcase. If we take that out—we'll have room for the couch."

With a carpenter's help, we completed the job quickly. Then all we had to do was wait.

From the moment it arrived, it has had a life all its own. It *vibrates* with vitality. It beckons to any passerby.

"Oh, that couch!" They reach out to connect with it, yet they hold back—as if in the presence of royalty. Aunt Sophia hasn't lost her touch!

So here I sit on my Lovely Lady, feeling her delicious energy course through me, before it radiates outward and fills up the room. She is more than just a memory or a photograph, she's my "touchstone to the past," a tangible thing. Her Victorian contours look strange with my stark white furniture—yet—somehow she fits in.

Stanley comes into the room and sits down beside me. "This couch is perfect!" he declares. On his face is the peculiar mixture of awe and excitement I have come to connect with this incredible piece of furniture. In a softer voice he adds, "It's a miracle. It was *Bashert*!"

We Remember Them

At the rising of the sun and at its going down,
We remember them.

At the blowing of the wind and in the chill of winter,
We remember them.

At the opening of the buds and in the rebirth of spring,
We remember them.

At the blueness of the skies and in the warmth of summer,
We remember them.

At the rustling of the leaves and in the beauty of autumn,
We remember them.

At the beginning of the year and when it ends,
We remember them.

As long as we live, they too will live, for they are now a part of us,
As we remember them.

When we are lost and sick at heart,
We remember them.

We Remember Them

When we have joy we crave to share,
We remember them.

When we have decisions that are difficult to make,
We remember them.

When we have achievements that are based on their's,
We remember them.

As long as we live, they too will live, for they are now a part of us,
As we remember them.

Rabbi Jack Riemer and Rabbi Sylvan Kamens
Reprinted with the kind permission of the authors

Bubby and I, when we were both young.

Jo-Ann Middleman was born and raised in Baltimore City. She lives now in San Diego with her husband Stanley—only two hours from her daughters Missy and Sharon (who's married to Steve) and four *delicious* grandchildren: Max, Jesse, Micah and Ilana.